WORLD HISTORY

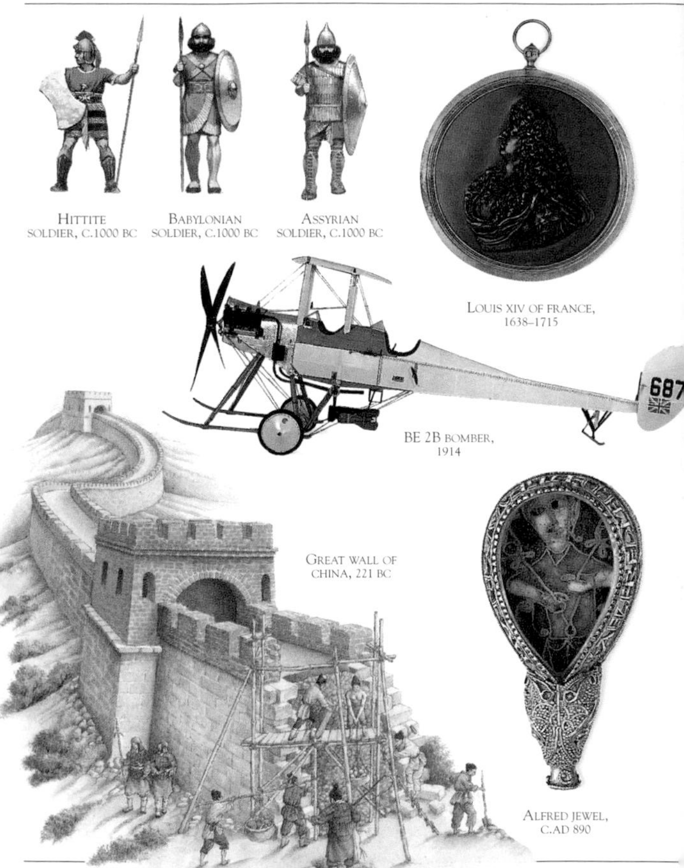

HITTITE SOLDIER, C.1000 BC

BABYLONIAN SOLDIER, C.1000 BC

ASSYRIAN SOLDIER, C.1000 BC

LOUIS XIV OF FRANCE, 1638–1715

BE 2B BOMBER, 1914

GREAT WALL OF CHINA, 221 BC

ALFRED JEWEL, C.AD 890

P • O • C • K • E • T • S

WORLD HISTORY

Written by
PHILIP WILKINSON

MAP OF VIKING TRAVELS

MODEL OF ROMAN CORBITA

DORLING KINDERSLEY
London • New York • Stuttgart

A DORLING KINDERSLEY BOOK

Project editor Claire Watts
Designer Kate Eagar
Art editors Carole Oliver
Sarah Ponder
Senior editor Hazel Egerton
Senior art editor Jacquie Gulliver
Researcher Robert Graham
Picture research Sharon Southren
Production Josie Alabaster

First published in Great Britain in 1996
by Dorling Kindersley Limited
9 Henrietta Street, Covent Garden, London WC2E 8PS

A CIP catalogue record for this book is available from the British Library.

ISBN 0 7513 5369 8

Colour reproduction by Colourscan, Singapore
Printed and bound in Italy by L.E.G.O.

Contents

HOW TO USE THIS BOOK

These pages show you how to use *Pockets: World History*. The book is divided into six sections covering different historical periods or events, and there is a reference section at the end. Each new section begins with a contents page and one or more time charts.

HEADING AND INTRODUCTION

The heading describes the subject of a page. If a subject continues over more than one page, the same heading applies. Some pages are divided further by subheadings. The introduction follows, and provides an overview of the subject.

CHARTS

Some pages have helpful charts that give a clear summary of information, such as major events, key dates, characters, or inventions.

FACT BOXES

Many pages contain fact boxes, coloured yellow. These boxes give at-a-glance information and provide extra facts about the subject.

Heading
Timeline
Introduction
Caption
Annotation
Feature box

THE HUNDRED YEARS WAR

ABBREVIATIONS USED IN THIS BOOK	
AD	Anno Domini
b.	born
BC	before Christ
c.	circa (around)
d.	died
MYA	million years ago
YA	years ago

FEATURE BOXES

Feature boxes supply extra information about a subject or cover an event that was taking place elsewhere at the same time.

CAPTIONS, LABELS, AND ANNOTATIONS

Each illustration has a caption, and many have labels for extra clarity. Annotations in *italics* give details about the picture.

TIMELINES AND COLOUR CODING

At the top of each text page, you will find a yellow timeline with a contrasting part. The dates at each end of the line refer to the section you are in. The part marked in a contrasting colour refers to the period covered by the page you are on.

3 MYA TO 5000 BC

5000 BC TO AD 600

600 TO 1400

1400 TO 1750

1750 TO 1900

1900 TO 1990s

TIME CHARTS

At the beginning of each section, you will find illustrated time charts. You can use these to compare events that were happening at the same time. The symbol ➡ means that you will find more information about the entry on the page indicated.

MAPS

Map *Subheading*

Many pages contain maps. These may show where particular civilizations lived, or what areas they travelled to. The map on this page illustrates how the Black Death spread across Europe.

REFERENCE SECTION, GLOSSARY, AND INDEX

At the back of the book, a reference section lists important world rulers, a glossary explains difficult words used in the book, and an index lists every subject in the book.

WHAT IS HISTORY?

FOR ALMOST AS LONG as people have been able to write, they have been writing about the past. Historians look at all sorts of different aspects of the past – rulers and governments, wars and battles, and the daily lives of ordinary people.

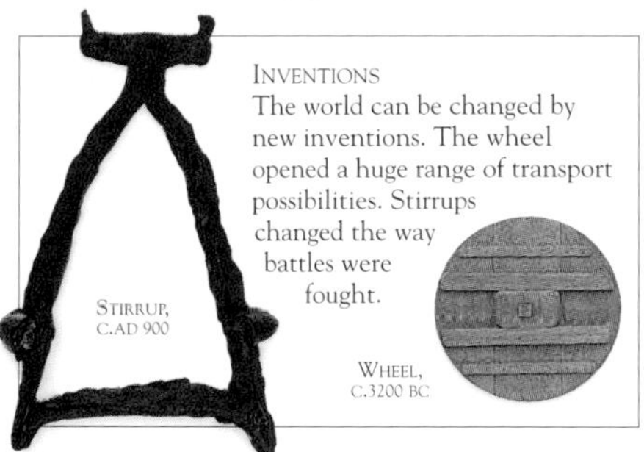

INVENTIONS
The world can be changed by new inventions. The wheel opened a huge range of transport possibilities. Stirrups changed the way battles were fought.

STIRRUP, C.AD 900

WHEEL, C.3200 BC

ANCIENT EGYPTIAN MUMMY

WHY DID THEY DO THAT?
Many of the things people did in the past seem very odd today. Historians try to work out why people did certain things, for example, why the Egyptians made mummies.

FAMOUS HISTORIANS

NAME	DATE	INFORMATION
Herodotus	c.484–c.425 BC	Greek "father of history"; wrote about the military and political history of the ancient world.
Bede	c.672–735	English historian who wrote a well-researched account of the English church and people.
Francesco Guicciardini	1483–1540	Italian historian who wrote eyewitness accounts of events that he had lived through.
Edward Gibbon	1737–1794	English historian who analysed the patterns of events, especially the fall of the Roman Empire.
Fernand Braudel	1902–1985	French historian who began to look at economic factors and the lives of ordinary people.

Picture of the past

Historians study a range of evidence and interpret it to build up a picture of the past. A historian studying the life of a medieval knight would look at documents, buildings, and archaeological artefacts to gain a complete view of the subject.

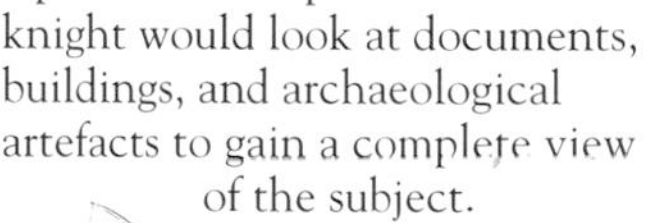

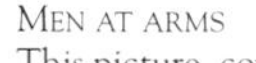

MEN AT ARMS
This picture, copied from a drawing done at the time, shows that archers aimed their bows high.

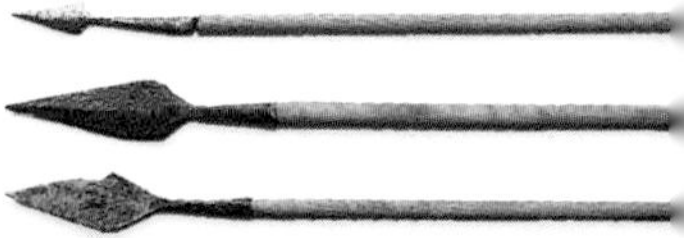

WEAPONS OF WAR
Medieval arrowheads unearthed by archaeologists show that the arrows were sharp enough to pierce armour.

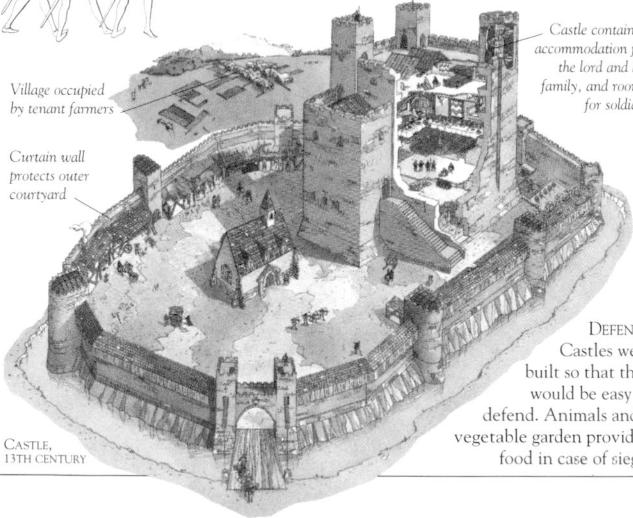

Castle contained accommodation for the lord and his family, and rooms for soldiers

Village occupied by tenant farmers

Curtain wall protects outer courtyard

DEFENCE
Castles were built so that they would be easy to defend. Animals and a vegetable garden provided food in case of siege.

CASTLE, 13TH CENTURY

HISTORICAL EVIDENCE

EVERYTHING, FROM AN old document to a building, a priceless jewel to a piece of litter, can provide clues about the past. This evidence can show us where people lived, what they did, and what was important to them. Interpreting evidence is the most fascinating part of the historian's job.

Inscription

ALFRED JEWEL, C.890

LUXURY ARTEFACTS
Richly decorated artefacts provide evidence about their period, such as the clothes people wore, the skill of craft-workers, and people's wealth.

VIKING COMB, 800S

Carved from elk antler

EVERYDAY ARTEFACTS
Simple items like this Viking comb can be very revealing. The discoveries of many combs show that appearance and health were important to the Vikings.

BUILDINGS
Architecture can provide fascinating historical evidence. The Colosseum tells us much about Roman life. The seats of different ranks of Roman society, the cages of the animals, and the cells of the gladiators can all be seen among the ruins.

COLOSSEUM, ROME, AD 80

Historical documents

Written documents

All kinds of books and papers are useful to historians, from actual accounts of past events to texts that show the interests and beliefs of people in the past.

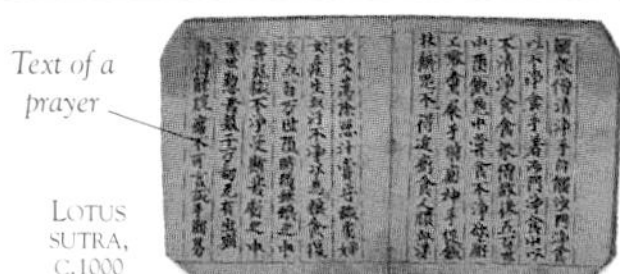

Text of a prayer

Lotus sutra, c.1000

Carved words

Texts are not always written in the form of books or scrolls. Over the years, people have used bone, silk, copper, stone, and wood to write on.

Runic inscription, Greenland, c.1000

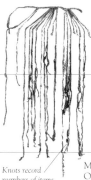

Records without writing

Even cultures that never developed writing invented their own ways of keeping records.

Inca quipu, c.1480

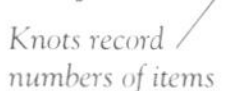

Knots record numbers of items

Maps

Old maps can show how much of the world was known to their makers, and which places were considered important.

Globe, c.1600

Modern newspapers

Making today's history

Modern historians use newspapers as an important source. They read as many accounts of an event as possible to try to get an overview of different opinions.

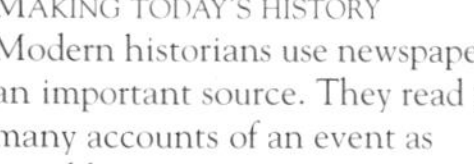

ARCHAEOLOGY

ARCHAEOLOGISTS study remains from the past – everything from fragments of pottery to human skeletons, from the foundations of old buildings to bits of industrial machinery. Modern archaeologists use scientific methods to analyse their finds and work out what life was like in the past.

HUMAN REMAINS
Human bones, like this skull from the Roman city of Herculaneum, can tell archaeologists how tall people were, what diseases they suffered from, and even what they usually ate.

EQUIPMENT AND TECHNIQUES

NAME	TOOL	INFORMATION
Trowel		Many archaeologists spend much of their time digging. Soil must be removed slowly and carefully, so as not to destroy any evidence.
Find bag		Every find is carefully recorded, numbered, bagged, and labelled. Recording is the most important of the archaeologist's jobs. Historians will be able to make full use of the finds only if the site and evidence are properly recorded.
Callipers		Each find must be measured. With delicate and irregular items, it can sometimes be difficult to use a tape measure, so callipers are used to gauge the exact size of the object.
Pole		Scale poles are placed next to objects that are photographed, so that it is easy to see how large the item is.

Interpreting the Landscape

High sun
No shadows

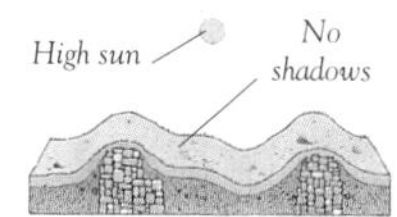

Noon

Remains of old buildings may appear as bumps on the surface. These are difficult to see when the sun is high in the sky.

Low sun
Shadows form

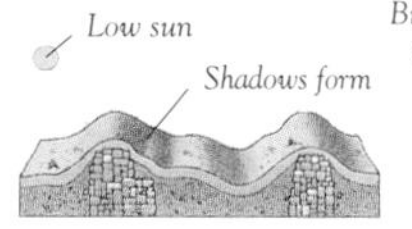

Sunset or Dawn

When the sun is low, the bumps can be seen more clearly, allowing archaeologists to work out what is underground.

Building stones stunt crops
Here, crops grow quickly

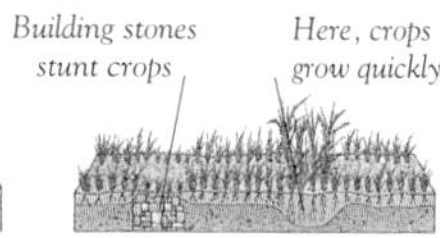

Crop Growth

Underground remains such as ditches or stones can affect crops. These differences can be seen easily from the air.

Excavation

Archaeologists carefully select a spot on an interesting site for an excavation or dig. When the topsoil has been removed, they gradually take away layers of soil, recording everything they find.

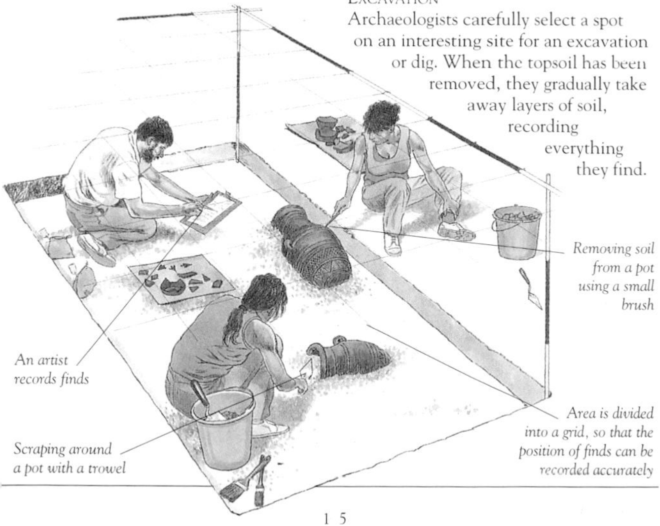

Removing soil from a pot using a small brush
An artist records finds
Area is divided into a grid, so that the position of finds can be recorded accurately
Scraping around a pot with a trowel

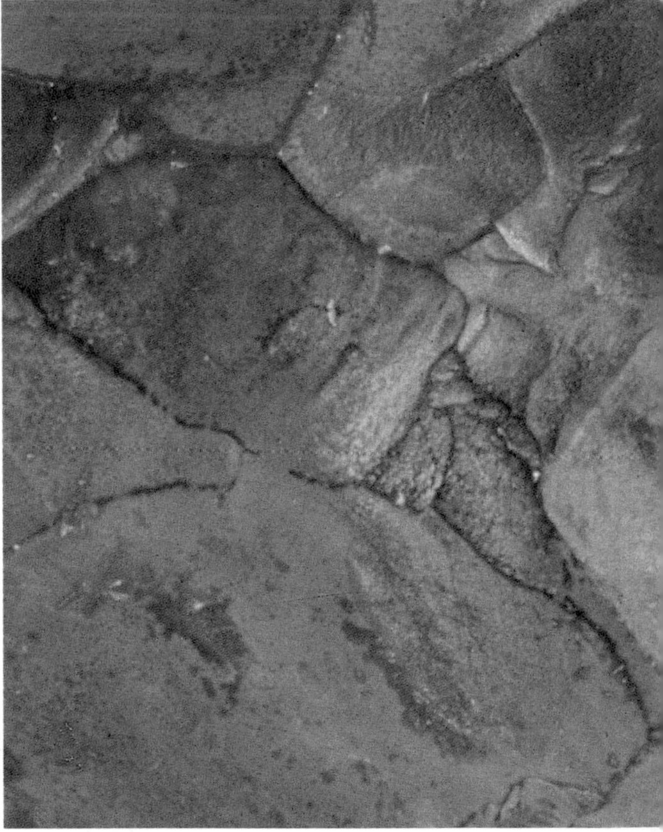

3 MYA TO 5000 BC

TIME CHART

	3 MYA	500,000 YA	50,000 BC
EVENTS	**3 MYA** *Australopithecus*, the first hominid to walk upright, appears in southern and eastern Africa ➡ 20 **2 MYA** *Homo habilis*, a tool-making hominid, appears in Africa **1.7 MYA** *Homo erectus* appears in eastern Africa ➡ 20 **1 MYA** *Homo erectus* has spread to eastern Asia and Java	**120,000 YA** Neanderthal people (*Homo sapiens neanderthalis*) appear in Europe and western Asia **100,000 YA** Modern humans (*Homo sapiens sapiens*) appear in Africa ➡ 20	**50,000 BC** Neanderthals present in western Europe, western Asia, and Uzbekistan **40,000 BC** Colonization of Australia by early *Homo sapiens sapiens* **40,000 BC** Cro-magnon man (early *Homo sapiens sapiens*) reaches Europe from Africa **30,000 YA** Beginning of last Ice Age ➡ 21 **30,000 BC** Neanderthals die out **25,000 BC** Start of coldest period of last Ice Age
ARTS & ARCHITECTURE		**450,000 YA** Simple stone windbreaks used for shelter, France **380,000 YA** Earliest known artificial shelter, France	**50,000 BC** Neanderthals engrave patterns on stone to make simple art objects **24,000 BC** Earliest known rock paintings, Africa **23,000 BC** Earliest known clay figures, Europe
SCIENCE & INVENTION	**3 MYA** Possible use of simple pebble tools ➡ 20, 21 **2 MYA** Simple stone tools used to make other tools **1.7 MYA** Handaxe first made; used as a general-purpose tool ➡ 20, 21	**460,000 YA** Earliest known use of fire, China **100,000 YA** Earliest known burials **100,000 YA** Specialized stone tools ➡ 21	**25,000 BC** Various methods of cooking food develop **24,000 BC** Earliest known cremation, Australia

MAMMOTH HUNT, 13,000 BC

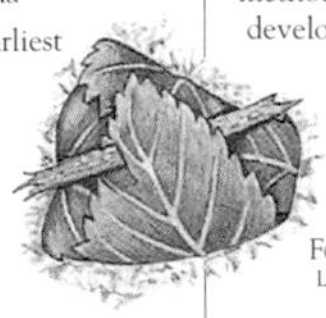

FOOD WRAPPED IN LEAVES, 25,000 BC

20,000 BC	12,000 BC	8000 BC
18,000 BC Coldest point of last Ice Age **18,000 BC** Settlement of Zaire, central Africa **17,000 BC** Wild cereal gathering, western Asia ➡ 22 **13,000 BC** Colonization of North America begins with the crossing of the land bridge between Asia and Alaska **13,000 BC** Ice-Age people hunt woolly mammoths ➡ 21 **13,000 BC** Rising sea levels submerge lowlands as the ice begins to thaw	FARMING, WESTERN ASIA 9000 BC  **11,000 BC** Colonization of South America begins with the arrival of people in Chile **10,000 BC** End of last Ice Age **9000 BC** Extinction of mammoth, perhaps due to over-hunting **9000 BC** Farming begins, western Asia ➡ 22, 23 **9000 BC** First people reach tip of South America	**8000 BC** Settlement of Jericho ➡ 24, 25 **6000 BC** Cattle domesticated, Sahara **6000 BC** New Guinea and Tasmania are cut off from Australia as sea level rises
20,000 BC–10,000 BC Cave paintings produced, France and Spain **16,000 BC** Mammoth-bone huts built, Europe 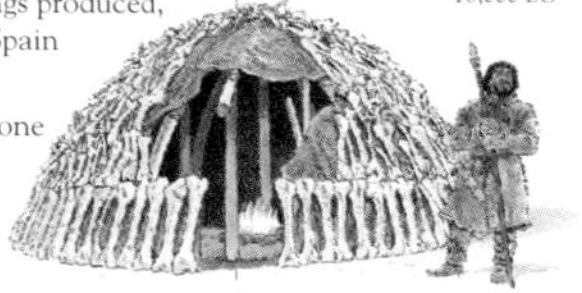	MAMMOTH-BONE HUT, 16,000 BC	**8000 BC** First large buildings of sun-dried bricks, western Asia **C.7000 BC** Animal carvings made in bone, antler, and amber, Denmark and southern Sweden
18,000 BC Bone needles used, Australia 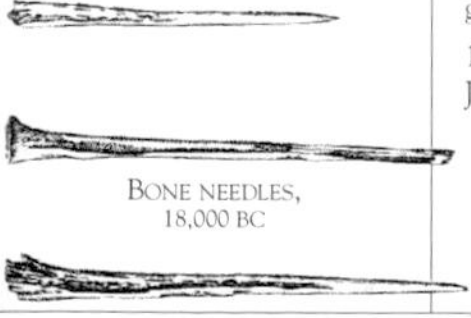 BONE NEEDLES, 18,000 BC	**11,000 BC** Tools made from obsidian, a black volcanic glass, Greece **10,500 BC** First pottery, Japan ➡ 25 **9000 BC** First sun-dried mud bricks, western Asia	**7500 BC** Earliest known cemetery, North America **7000 BC** Early metal-working using raw copper and gold nuggets beaten into shape, western Asia **7000 BC** Stone spade first used, China

EARLY PEOPLE

FOSSIL REMAINS SHOW that two million years ago several species of human-like creatures (hominids) existed at the same time. Gradually, more intelligent and skilful species of hominids developed, and older species died out. Then, about 100,000 years ago, the first true humans (*Homo sapiens sapiens*) appeared.

BRAINS AND SKULLS

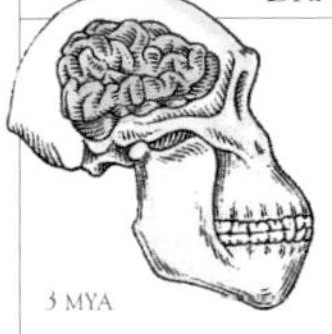
3 MYA

AUSTRALOPITHECUS

These creatures lived in Africa and were probably the first primates to walk upright. They had small brains, long arms, and large, powerful jaws with strong teeth.

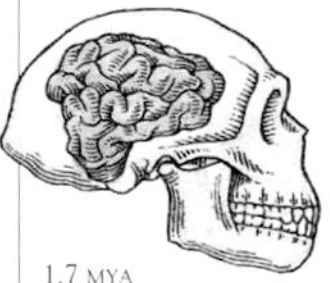
1.7 MYA

HOMO ERECTUS

This species had larger skulls than previous hominids. They invented the handaxe, a sharp cutting or chopping tool, and learned to make fire.

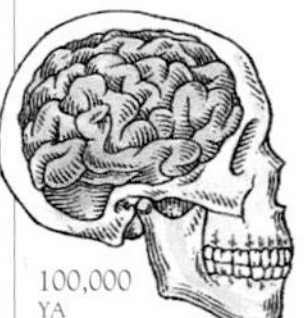
100,000 YA

HOMO SAPIENS SAPIENS

Our own ancestors were skilful tool-makers and hunter-gatherers. By about 35,000 years ago, they had spread all over Europe and reached Australia.

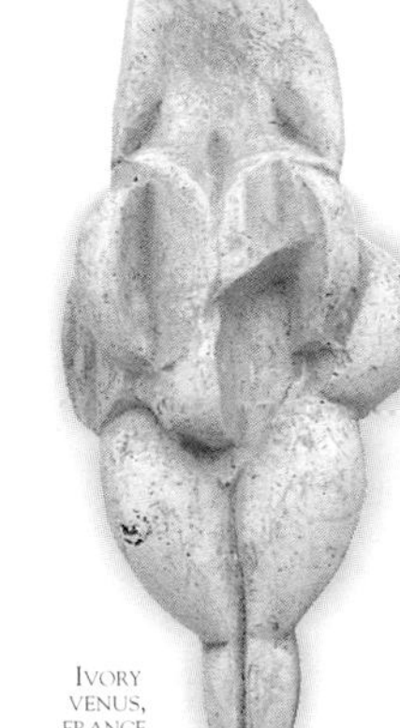
Early female statues are always faceless

IVORY VENUS, FRANCE, C.25,000 YA

THE FIRST ART

Early people decorated caves with paintings of bison, wild cattle, and horses. They also produced small statuettes, often of female figures.

The Ice Age

The last Ice Age occurred between 30,000 BC and 10,000 BC. Much of the world was colder, the sea level was lower, and North Africa had a damp climate. People adapted well to these conditions. When they killed an animal, they used every part. The flesh was eaten, the skins made into clothes, and the bones used for tools.

Covered pit to trap the mammoth
Stones were used to stun the mammoth

Wooden spear with flint blade

Coat made from animal skins

MAMMOTH HUNT

FOOD SUPPLY

In spring, summer, and autumn, people gathered plant foods to eat, but in winter, they relied on meat. They usually hunted in groups, and then shared the kill among the hunters.

TECHNOLOGY

HANDAXE

FLINT SCRAPER

BOW AND ARROWS

Sharp stone arrowhead

Bows and arrows appeared in Africa between 30,000 and 15,000 BC. In Europe and Asia, spears and harpoons were used. As well as the handaxe, a range of more specialized tools was also produced.

ITEM	FUNCTION	FOUND
	Comb	Mesopotamia
	Needle	Eastern Mediterranean
	Harpoon	Europe
	Fish hook	Europe
	Beads	Eastern Mediterranean

SETTLERS AND FARMERS

AROUND 11,000 BC, the ice caps were retreating northwards, bringing about climate changes and making the land more fertile. People in some parts of the world began to give up their wandering hunter-gatherer lifestyle and settle down. By 9000 BC, people had learned to plant and harvest cereal crops and to domesticate animals.

NATUFIAN SETTLEMENT

SETTLING DOWN

The Natufian people of Palestine were one of the first groups to live in permanent settlements. Some lived in caves, others built huts of mud, reeds, and timber. The first Natufians gathered wild grain and stored it in their huts.

CROP CULTIVATION

Wild wheat, such as emmer and einkorn, is difficult to harvest because the ripe seed heads shatter. Early farmers combined existing varieties to develop better types of wheat.

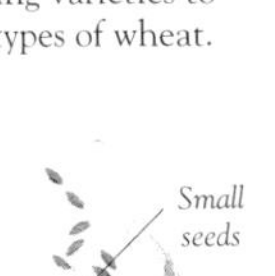

Seed head easier to harvest

Small seeds

Wild emmer has small seeds

Domestic emmer has large seeds

Ripe seed head shatters

DOMESTIC EMMER

WILD EMMER

DOMESTIC EINKORN

WILD EINKORN

ANIMAL DOMESTICATION

Farmers gradually learned to breed farm animals that produced more meat, wool, or milk than their wild ancestors.

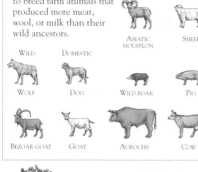

WILD DOMESTIC

ASIATIC MOUFLON

SHEEP

WILD DOMESTIC

WOLF

DOG

WILD BOAR

PIG

BEZOAR GOAT

GOAT

AUROCHS

COW

HUNTER-GATHERERS

- In many parts of the world people kept to hunter-gatherer lifestyles because there was plenty of wild food available.
- They developed specialized hunting tools and weapons.
- Some people still live by hunting and gathering today, in Africa, Australia, and South America.

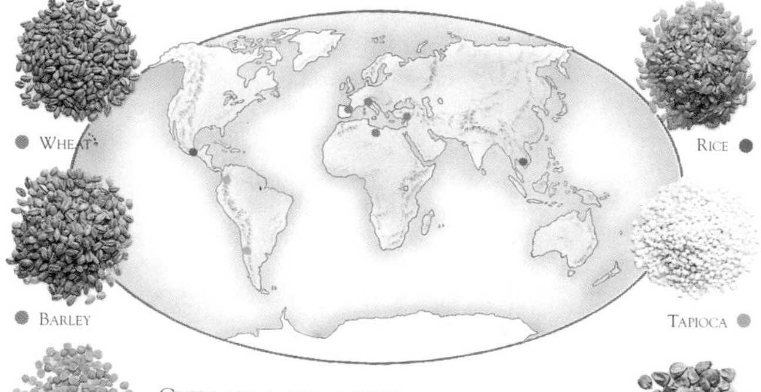
WHEAT

BARLEY

RICE

TAPIOCA

LENTILS

CROPS AROUND THE WORLD

From its beginnings in western Asia, farming spread to Europe and central Asia. Elsewhere, agriculture developed independently when crops were cultivated from local wild plants.

MAIZE

TOWNS AND TRADE

AS PEOPLE BEGAN to settle in groups, they found that they could specialize – some people farmed, while others made tools and pots. Villages began to produce more food and goods than they needed for themselves. They traded this surplus with other villages. The most successful trading communities grew into the first towns.

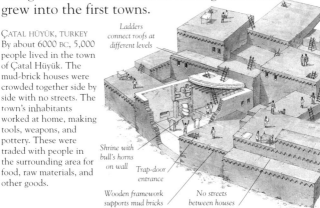

ÇATAL HÜYÜK, TURKEY
By about 6000 BC, 5,000 people lived in the town of Çatal Hüyük. The mud-brick houses were crowded together side by side with no streets. The town's inhabitants worked at home, making tools, weapons, and pottery. These were traded with people in the surrounding area for food, raw materials, and other goods.

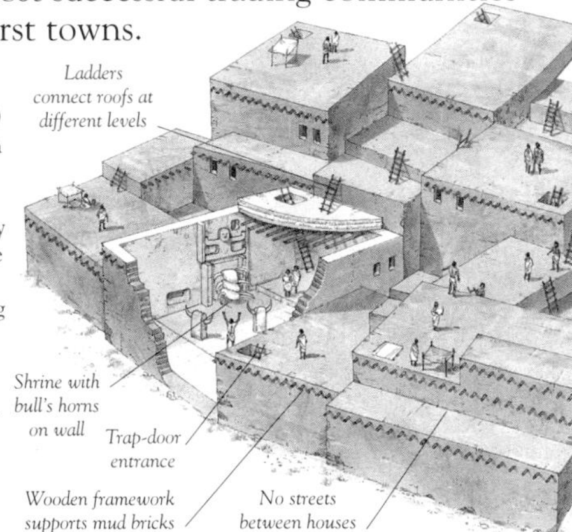

EARLY TOWNS			
TOWN	AREA	DATE	MAIN CRAFT
Jericho	Eastern Mediterranean	8000 BC	Pottery
Çatal Hüyük	Turkey	7000 BC	Pottery and obsidian tools
Jarmo	Iraq	7000 BC	Textiles
Khirokitia	Cyprus	6000 BC	Stone and wood items
Ugarit	Eastern Mediterranean	6000 BC	Textiles

Ideas and innovations

Decorated pot, Germany, c.6000 BC

Pottery

The art of pottery was first developed in Japan in about 10,500 BC. Pots were usually made by coiling a snake-like length of clay in a spiral, and then smoothing down the surface.

Spinning

Wool was twisted into a strong thread using a wooden spindle. This could be woven to make warm cloth.

Metal-working

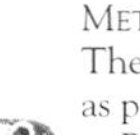
Casting, or pouring molten metal into a mould

The first metals were found as pure lumps that could be beaten into shape. By 6500 BC, people had discovered how to extract metals from rocks.

Marks of ownership

People in the early towns used clay stamps to mark personal property and trade-goods. The seal was pushed into wet clay, which made a permanent mark when it set hard.

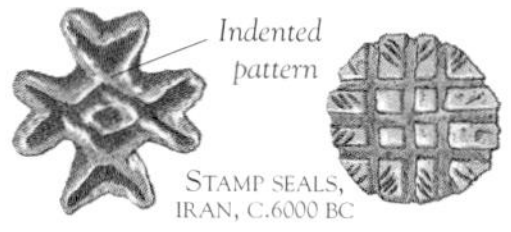

Stamp seals, Iran, c.6000 BC

First religion

Early towns were often religious centres. The people of Jericho decorated human skulls for use in their religious rituals.

Plastered skull, Jericho, c.8000 BC

Bread-making

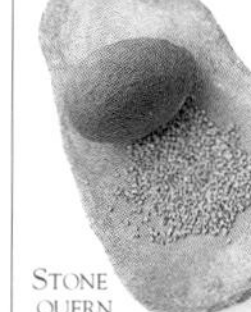
Stone quern

Grain was ground on a stone quern to make flour. This was then mixed with water, and baked in a dome-shaped clay oven to make unleavened (yeastless) bread. Once the dough was inside the oven, the entrance was blocked up with clay to keep in the heat.

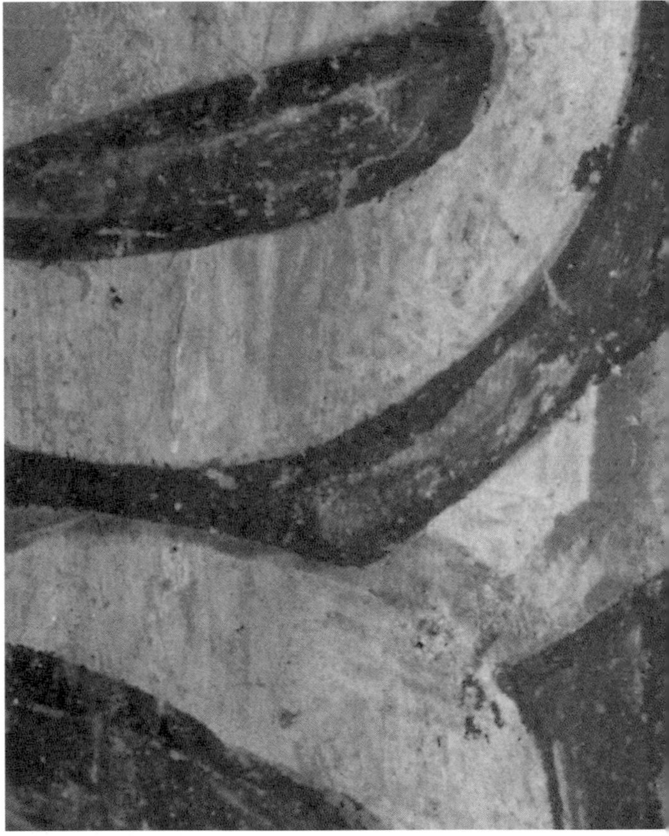

5000 BC TO AD 600

TIME CHART

	5000 BC	4000 BC	3000 BC
EVENTS	**5000 BC** First cities are founded in Mesopotamia, western Asia ➡ 32, 33 **5000 BC** First settlements in Anahuac, Mexico **5000 BC** Maize first cultivated, Mexico **5000 BC** Rice first cultivated, China **4500 BC** Farming begins around River Ganges, India **4400 BC** Horses domesticated, Russia	ANIMALS DOMESTICATED, SAHARA, 4000 BC **4000 BC** Farming communities begin to domesticate animals, Sahara **3500 BC** City of Ur founded, Mesopotamia ➡ 32 **3500 BC** Earliest Chinese city, Liang-ch'eng chen, founded **c.3100 BC** Menes unites Upper and Lower Egypt	**3000 BC** Bronze age begins, Crete **2750 BC** Gilgamesh becomes King of Sumer **2686 BC–2182 BC** Old Kingdom period, Egypt **2500 BC** Sahara region begins to dry out **2330 BC** Sargon of Akkad (d.2275) dominates Sumer ➡ 33 **2300 BC** Beginning of Indus Valley civilization, Pakistan ➡ 33 **2133 BC–1786 BC** Middle Kingdom period, Egypt
ARTS & ARCHITECTURE	**5000 BC** First ziggurats built, Sumer ➡ 32 **4500 BC** Cave art flourishes, northern Africa **4500 BC** First megalithic tombs built, Britain and Portugal **4500 BC** Passage graves built, France	**4000 BC** Pyramid temples, Peru STONEHENGE, 2800 BC	**2800 BC** Building starts on Stonehenge, England **c.2646 BC** Building of Pyramid of Zoser, Egypt ➡ 34 **c.2590 BC** Building of Pyramid of Khufu, Egypt ➡ 34
SCIENCE & INVENTION	**5000 BC** Copper first used, Mesopotamia **5000 BC** Irrigation systems used, Mesopotamia SOWING RICE, CHINA, 5000 BC	**3500 BC** Plough and wheel used, Mesopotamia ➡ 33 **3500 BC** Sailing boats used on the Nile, Egypt ➡ 35 **3250 BC** Development of cuneiform, Mesopotamia ➡ 33	**3000 BC** Day divided into 24 hours, Babylon **3000 BC** Development of hieroglyphic script, Egypt ➡ 35 **2500 BC** Standard weights first used, Mesopotamia

2000 BC	1550 BC	1100 BC
2000 BC End of Sumerian power in Mesopotamia **c.1790 BC** Hammurabi (1792 BC–1750 BC) becomes King of Babylon → 38 **1595 BC** Hittites sack Babylon **1567 BC–1085 BC** New Kingdom, Egypt  HAMMURABI	**c.1500 BC** Collapse of Minoan civilization **1300 BC** Rise of Olmec civilization, Mexico **1279 BC** Rameses II (1290 BC–1213 BC) becomes pharaoh of Egypt → 34 **1218 BC** Egypt and Eastern Mediterranean invaded by Sea Peoples from the Aegean **1200 BC** Collapse of Hittite empire **1200 BC** Greeks destroy city of Troy after ten-year war **1200 BC** Jews settle in Palestine **1120 BC** Mycenae destroyed	**1100 BC** Rise of Phoenician civilization, eastern Mediterranean → 36, 37 **c.970 BC** Solomon becomes King of Israel **900 BC** State of Sparta founded, Greece **814 BC** City of Carthage founded, North Africa **800 BC** Etruscan people establish city-states, western Italy → 36, 37 **776 BC** First Olympic Games held, Greece **753 BC** Rome founded **604 BC** Nebuchadnezzar II (d.562 BC) becomes King of Babylon → 39
2000 BC Minoan palaces built, Crete → 36, 37 **1600 BC** Mycenaean citadels built, Greece → 37	**1200 BC** Enamel used to decorate mummy cases MINOAN PALACE, 2000 BC	**973 BC** Solomon orders building of temple of Jerusalem **800 BC–700 BC** Homer writes the *Odyssey* and the *Iliad* **605–562 BC** Hanging gardens constructed, Babylon → 39
2000 BC Chariot first used, Mesopotamia → 38, 39 **1900 BC** Iron smelting, Mesopotamia **1700 BC** Early alphabetic script developed, Phoenicia	**1500 BC** Silk fabric first made, China **1450 BC** First shadow clocks, Egypt  MESOPOTAMIAN CHARIOT 2000 BC	**620 BC** Coins first used, Asia

Time Chart

	600 BC	400 BC	200 BC
EVENTS	**563 BC–483 BC** Life of Buddha ➡ 43 **557 BC** Cyrus (d.529 BC) becomes King of Persia, and founds Persian Empire **551 BC–479 BC** Life of Confucius **510 BC** Roman Republic founded **500 BC** Beginning of iron-working Nok culture, Nigeria **490 BC** Battle of Marathon, Greece ➡ 41 **431 BC–404 BC** Peloponnesian Wars, Greece ➡ 41	**334 BC–326 BC** Alexander the Great (356 BC–323 BC) conquers much of Asia ➡ 41 **322 BC** Chandragupta Maurya founds Mauryan Empire, India ➡ 42 **264 BC–146 BC** Punic Wars between Rome and Carthage **221 BC** Unification of China ➡ 44 **216 BC** Roman army defeated by Hannibal (247 BC–183 BC) at Cannae	**147 BC–6 BC** Greece comes under Roman rule **49 BC** Julius Caesar (100 BC–44 BC) invades Gaul **46 BC** Caesar becomes Roman Dictator ➡ 47 **30 BC** Cleopatra (b.69 BC), ruler of Egypt, commits suicide **27 BC** Augustus (63 BC–AD 14) becomes first Roman Emperor ➡ 46 **c.4 BC–AD 30** Life of Jesus Christ ➡ 48 ROMAN SOLDIERS, 264 BC
ARTS & ARCHITECTURE	**600 BC** Temple of the Sun built, Meroë, Sudan **560 BC** Lao-Tzu (c.604 BC–c.531 BC) writes his philosophical work, *Tao Te Ching*, China **460 BC** Start of golden age of art and architecture, Greece	**290 BC** Foundation of library, Alexandria, Egypt **285 BC** Earliest known lighthouse, Pharos, Egypt **221 BC** Building starts on Great Wall of China ➡ 44	**100 BC** Terracotta art flourishes, India **30–19 BC** Virgil (70–19) writes the *Aeneid* GREAT WALL OF CHINA, 221 BC
SCIENCE & INVENTION	**550 BC** Maps first used by travellers **500 BC** Greeks develop oar-powered warship **500 BC** Persians begin to build road network **450 BC** Abacus used, Mediterranean	**400 BC** Hippocrates (460 BC–377 BC) sets up medical school, Greece **300 BC** Water clock invented, Egypt **230 BC** Earliest known metal springs, Alexandria, Egypt	**100 BC** Glass-blowing invented, Syria **100 BC** Stirrups first used, India **85 BC** Water-powered mill used for grinding grain, Greece

AD 1	AD 300	AD 400
AD 1 Beginning of Moche civilization, Peru **AD 43** Romans invade Britain **AD 50** Kingdom of Axum begins to expand, Ethiopia **AD 50** Buddhism reaches China ➡ 43 **AD 60–61** Rebellion of Boudicca (d.AD 61) against Romans in Britain **AD 79** Eruption of Vesuvius destroys Pompeii, Italy **AD 193** Septimius Severus (146–211) becomes Roman Emperor	**212** Roman citizenship extended to all free-born people in the empire **220** End of Han dynasty, China ➡ 45 **235–84** Period of civil war in Roman Empire **284–305** Emperor Diocletian (245–313) restores order to Rome ➡ 47 **311** Constantine (280–337) proclaimed Roman Emperor ➡ 48 **360s** First invasion of Europe by Huns from Asia **330** Foundation of Constantinople ➡ 49	**400s** Christianity becomes widespread in Axum Empire, northeast Africa ➡ 48 **410** Visigoths sack Rome **445** Attila the Hun (406–453) attacks western Europe **500** Hopewell culture at its peak, North America ➡ 51 **527** Justinian I (483–565) becomes Byzantine Emperor ➡ 49 **550** Buddhism introduced to Japan ➡ 43 **570–632** Life of Muhammad ➡ 58
AD 50 Nazca culture flourishes in Peru; Nazca people create vast lines and patterns in the desert **AD 80** Colosseum opened, Rome **AD 122–138** Hadrian's Wall built, Britain	**397–401** St Augustine (354–430) writes his *Confessions* 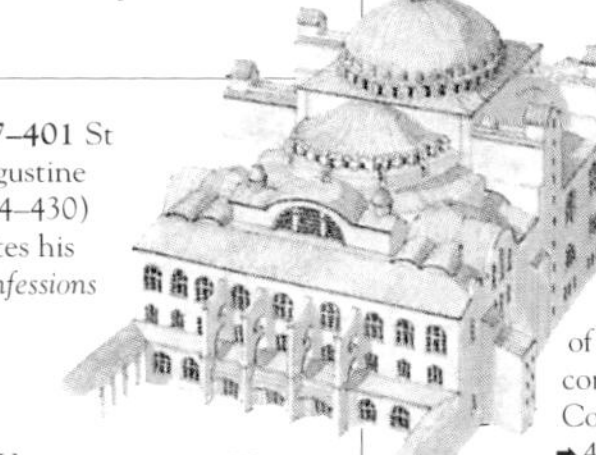 HAGIA SOPHIA, AD 537	**537** Church of Hagia Sophia completed, Constantinople ➡ 49
AD 50 Horseshoe first used, Italy **AD 100** Concrete used for building, Rome **AD 105** Paper invented, China ➡ 44	**200** Cast iron invented, China  PAPER, CHINA, AD 105	**500** Indian mathematicians introduce the zero **500** Stencil used for text, China and Japan **599** Chess invented, India

The First Cities

THE EARLIEST CITIES grew up in Mesopotamia, the area between the Tigris and Euphrates rivers. The land was fertile, so people grew grain and raised animals. The Sumerians (the people of Mesopotamia) traded grain with nearby areas, getting metals and tools in return. Different cities dominated the region at different times, but they all had a similar culture.

Temples

The Sumerians had an organized religion with many different gods. Each city had a ziggurat (temple) consisting of a series of platforms with stairs. The ziggurat at Ur, built in about 2100 BC, was dedicated to the moon god Nanna, who was the city's local god. The priests made offerings to the god every day.

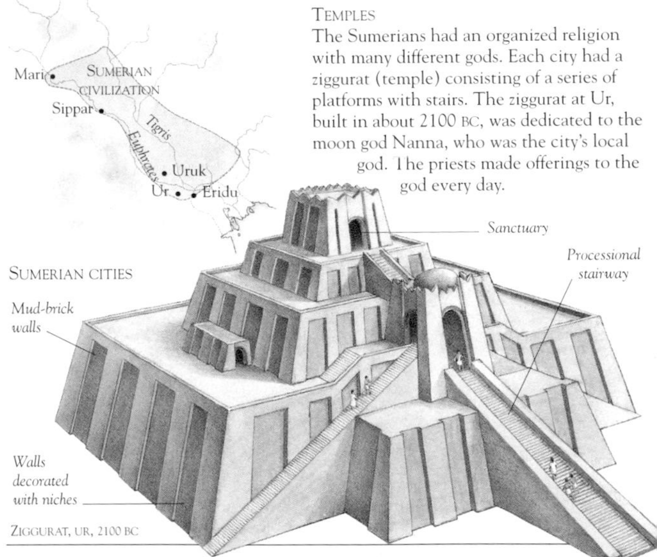

SUMERIAN CITIES

ZIGGURAT, UR, 2100 BC

CUNEIFORM

The first picture-writing gradually developed into the cuneiform script used by the Sumerians. They used a reed to make marks in damp clay.

Record of foundation of building

FOUNDATION STONE, UR, C.2300 BC

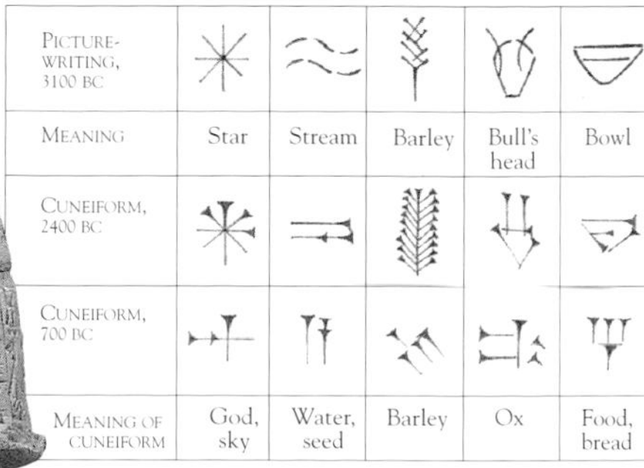

PICTURE-WRITING, 3100 BC					
MEANING	Star	Stream	Barley	Bull's head	Bowl
CUNEIFORM, 2400 BC					
CUNEIFORM, 700 BC					
MEANING OF CUNEIFORM	God, sky	Water, seed	Barley	Ox	Food, bread

KINGS

Each city was ruled by a king with a team of priests. In c.2330 BC, Sargon II, King of Akkad, brought the whole of Mesopotamia under his rule.

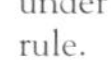

INVENTIONS

As well as the first writing system, the Sumerians invented the plough to improve agriculture, and the wheel to make transport easier.

WRITING

PLOUGH

WHEEL

Kings often had elaborate hairstyles

Cast bronze

Curled beard

SARGON II OF AKKAD

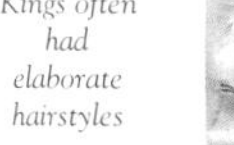

BULL SEAL

IMPRESSION

INDUS VALLEY CIVILIZATION

Cities were also built near the Indus river between 2300 BC and 1750 BC. Indus Valley people used seals to show ownership of property.

Ancient Egypt

THE CIVILIZATION OF ancient Egypt flourished for more than 3,000 years along the banks of the Nile. The country was ruled by pharaohs (kings) who had absolute power and were thought to become gods when they died. The Egyptians traded with other parts of Africa, Asia, and the Mediterranean.

Famous Pharaohs

- Zoser (c.2700 BC) built the first pyramid, the Step Pyramid at Saqqara.
- Hatshepsut (c.1473 BC–1458 BC) was the world's first recorded female ruler.
- Rameses II (1290 BC–1213 BC) built new temples and conquered new territory.

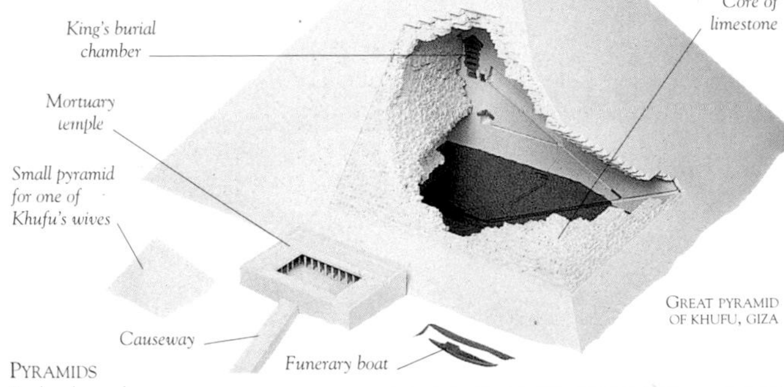

GREAT PYRAMID OF KHUFU, GIZA

Pyramids

Early pharaohs were buried in pyramids with all the possessions that the Egyptians thought they would need in the afterlife. Thousands of people worked on the Great Pyramid, which took over 20 years to build.

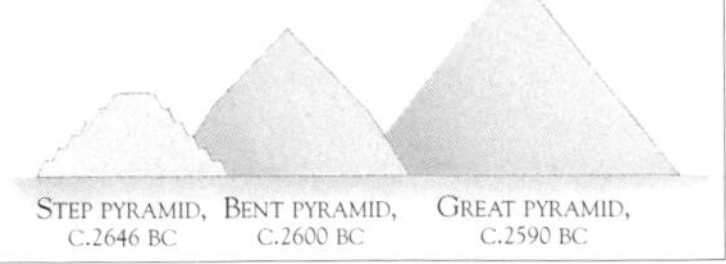
STEP PYRAMID, C.2646 BC BENT PYRAMID, C.2600 BC GREAT PYRAMID, C.2590 BC

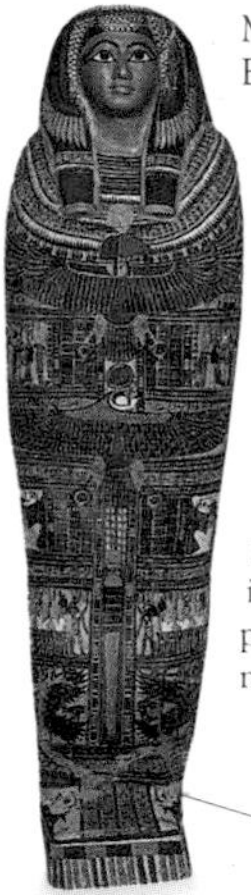

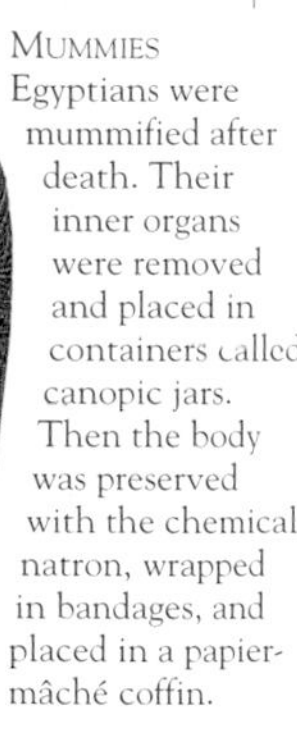

MUMMIES
Egyptians were mummified after death. Their inner organs were removed and placed in containers called canopic jars. Then the body was preserved with the chemical natron, wrapped in bandages, and placed in a papier-mâché coffin.

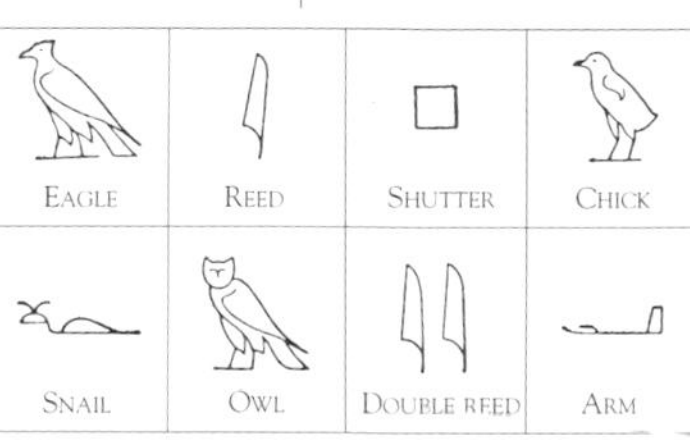

EGYPTIAN HIEROGLYPHS
The Egyptians developed their own system of writing. They wrote using hieroglyphs – simplified pictures that could represent sounds or actual objects. Scribes later developed two other scripts, hieratic and demotic, which were much simpler and quicker to write.

THE RIVER NILE
The Nile provided Egypt's main highway, along which everything from food to stone for the pyramids was carried. The Nile's yearly flooding also made the land fertile.

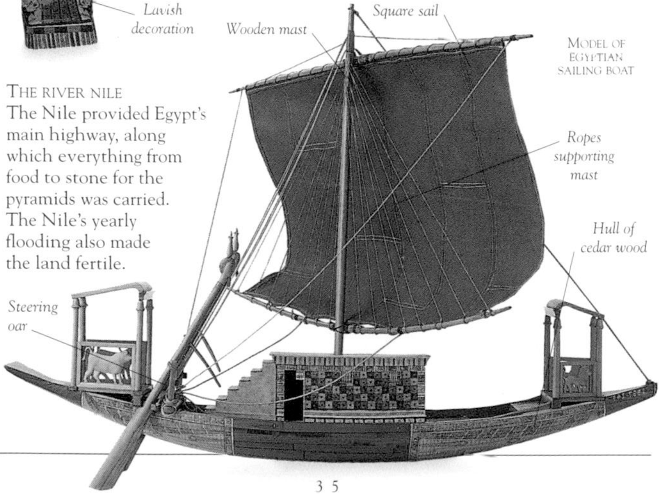

Square sail

Wooden mast

Ropes supporting mast

Hull of cedar wood

Steering oar

MODEL OF EGYPTIAN SAILING BOAT

MEDITERRANEAN POWERS

A GROUP OF PEOPLES dominated the Mediterranean in the second millennium BC. The Minoans, Mycenaeans, Phoenicians, and Etruscans lived in groups of city-states, and they all used trade to extend their influence. Each of these peoples had a typical style of arts and crafts, so modern archaeologists have been able to track their traders through objects found in different places around the Mediterranean.

THE ETRUSCANS
The Etruscans founded city-states in Italy in about 800 BC. They were renowned for their art and architecture. Little is known about the Etruscans' history, since their script has not yet been deciphered, but they were conquered by the Romans in the third century BC.

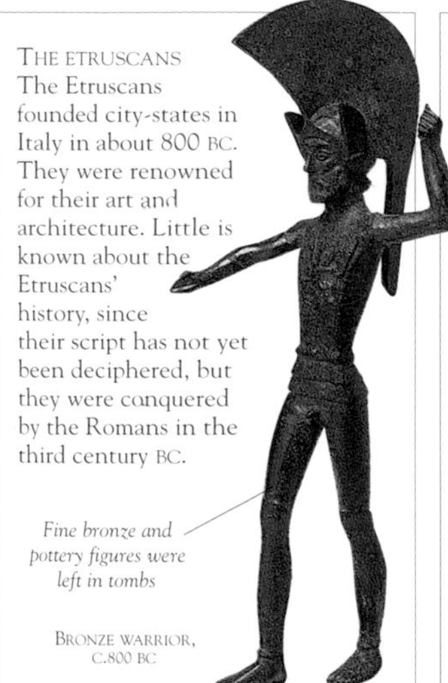

Fine bronze and pottery figures were left in tombs

BRONZE WARRIOR, C.800 BC

THE MINOANS
These people lived on the island of Crete. They traded grain, wine, and oil, and used the wealth they accumulated to build a series of huge palaces at Knossos, Mallia, Phaistos, and Zakro. Beautiful palace wall-paintings include scenes of people leaping over the horns of running bulls. No one knows why the Minoans did this, but it may have been part of a religious ritual.

STORAGE JAR, KNOSSOS, C.1500 BC

PAINTING OF BULL-LEAPING, KNOSSOS, C.1500 BC

MEDITERRANEAN CIVILIZATIONS

THE PHOENICIANS

Accomplished sailors, the Phoenicians travelled all over the Mediterranean, trading and founding cities as far away as Spain and North Africa. They made beautiful glassware and sculptures, which they sold to buy raw materials and slaves. The Phoenicians also developed a way of dyeing cloth purple using murex shells.

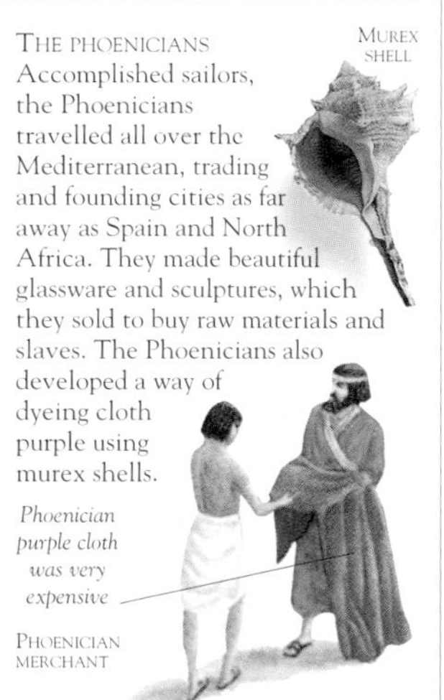

MUREX SHELL

Phoenician purple cloth was very expensive

PHOENICIAN MERCHANT

THE MYCENAEANS

The Mycenaeans dominated southern Greece and the Aegean Sea, and took over Crete when the Minoan civilization fell. They built towns with strong walls and small palaces for their kings.

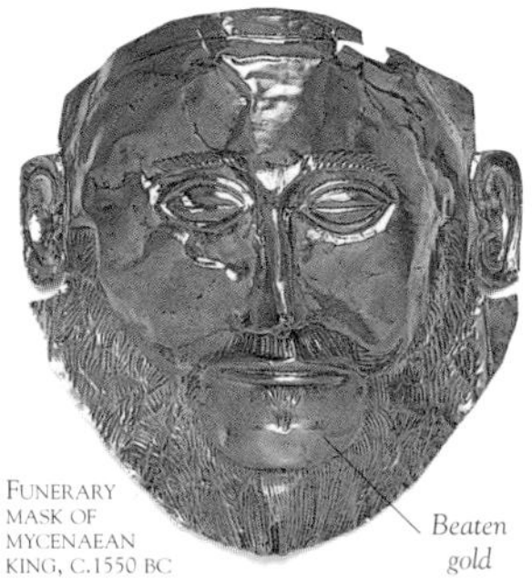

FUNERARY MASK OF MYCENAEAN KING, C.1550 BC

Beaten gold

Western Asia

THE CITY-STATES OF western Asia gradually expanded into empires. The Assyrians, Hittites, and Babylonians formed large armies to conquer their neighbours. The peoples who were defeated had to send their conquerors tributes of goods and money, which financed the building of large cities such as Babylon.

Hammurabi's laws

Hammurabi, King of Babylon (1792 BC–1750 BC) established a code of 282 laws. These laws included:

- If a man robbed another, the robber was put to death.
- If a son hit his father, his hand was cut off.
- If a man put out the eye of another, his eye was put out, too.

Soldiers of Western Asia

Assyrian soldier
In their armour made of metal scales, Assyrian soldiers were feared all over western Asia.

Hittite soldier
The Hittites were skilled with all weapons: bows and arrows, battle-axes, swords, and spears.

Babylonian soldier
Some Babylonian soldiers fought on foot, while others shot arrows from chariots.

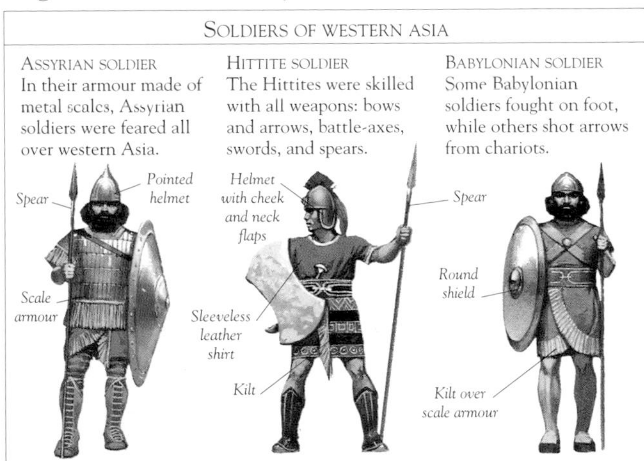

THE CITY OF BABYLON

In 605 BC, when King Nebuchadnezzar II (d.562 BC) ruled Babylon, he expanded the empire and rebuilt the city. He created the famous hanging gardens, and added a large new gate and an avenue called the Sacred Way leading to the palace and the temple.

HITTITE CHARIOTS

The Hittites used the chariot as a type of weapon. They drove through enemy lines at full speed, breaking up the ranks and causing chaos. Foot soldiers followed on, picking off the weakened enemy.

ASSYRIAN ART

The Assyrians decorated their palaces with huge carved stone reliefs of kings and gods. They also carved tiny ivory reliefs.

THE SACRED WAY, BABYLON, C.600 BC

ANCIENT GREECE

ANCIENT GREECE was not one country, but a series of city-states, each controlling lands in the surrounding area. The most powerful city-states were Athens and Sparta.

VOTING DISCS

DEMOCRACY
Decisions on how Athens was run were taken by a vote of male citizens. There was no vote for women or slaves.

GREEK VASES
The work of ancient Greek painters is preserved on many vases. Stories from Greek myths, animals, and scenes from daily life were popular subjects. This vase shows a scene from a symposium (banquet).

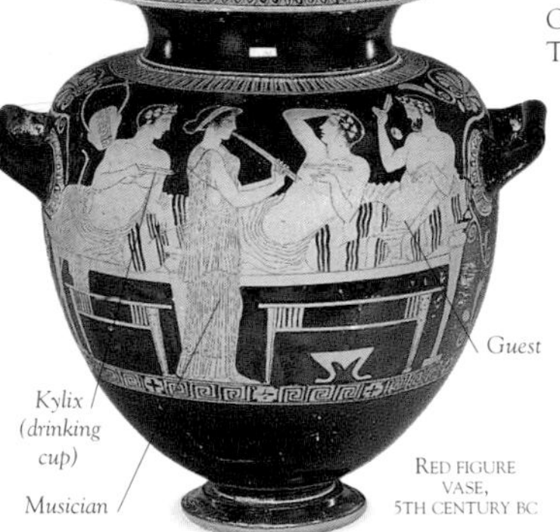

RED FIGURE VASE, 5TH CENTURY BC

FAMOUS PHILOSOPHERS		
NAME	DATES	INTEREST
Socrates	469 BC–399 BC	Studied the principles that govern human life.
Plato	c.427 BC–347 BC	Wrote dialogues featuring his master, Socrates.
Aristotle	384 BC–322 BC	Concentrated on how the world works.

GREEK GODS
The Greeks worshipped many gods, who were believed to live on Mount Olympus in northern Greece. Many Greek myths and plays told stories about the gods.

DEMETER, GODDESS OF FARMING

ZEUS, KING OF THE GODS

COLUMNS

These columns are typical of the three styles of Greek architecture.

GREEK WARS

Athens had to fight many challengers.

- The Greeks defeated Persian invaders at Marathon (490 BC) and Salamis (480 BC).
- In the Peloponnesian Wars (431 BC–404 BC), Sparta challenged and defeated Athens.

ARCHITECTURE

Greek cities had beautiful temples, theatres, and other public buildings. Some of the finest were built on the Acropolis, the hill overlooking the city of Athens.

Parthenon (temple of Athena)

Propylea (entrance to the Acropolis)

Theatre of Dionysus

Sanctuary of Asclepius

THE ACROPOLIS, ATHENS

EMPIRE OF ALEXANDER THE GREAT, 323 BC

ALEXANDER THE GREAT

Greece had a second heyday during the rule of the Macedonian Emperor Alexander the Great (356 BC–323 BC). His empire stretched as far as the Indus River, but it collapsed after his death.

THE RISE OF BUDDHISM

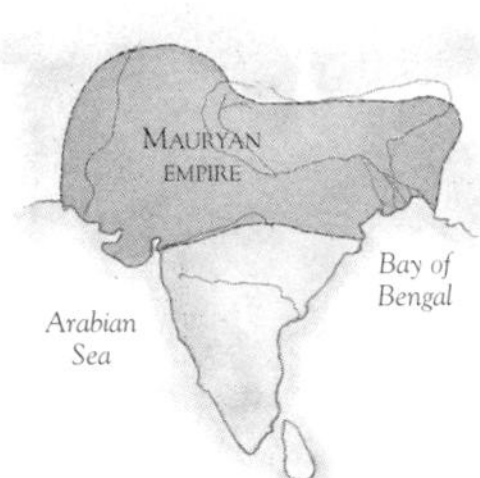

IN THE SIXTH CENTURY BC, the new, peaceful Buddhist faith appeared in India. To begin with, the principles of Buddhism spread slowly, but in the third century BC, the Indian Emperor Asoka (d.c.232 BC) became a Buddhist, and promoted the faith throughout his empire.

THE MAURYAN EMPIRE
Chandragupta Maurya led a revolt against Alexander the Great's governors in c.322 BC, and established a northern Indian nation. Chandragupta's grandson Asoka expanded the empire southwards.

CLASS SYSTEM

From the earliest times, Indian society has been divided into four separate classes.

- Brahmana, the privileged priest class.
- Kshatriya, the ruling warrior class.
- Vaisya, the merchant and land-owning class.
- Sudra, the servant or peasant class.

MAURYAN CARVING
The Mauryan period was a golden age of sculpture, during which local styles often blended with a Persian influence that had been introduced at the time of Alexander.

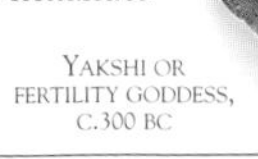
YAKSHI OR FERTILITY GODDESS, C.300 BC

The Buddha

Buddhism began when a young Indian nobleman, Siddhartha Gautama (563 BC–483 BC), left his life of luxury to find a way to deal with human suffering. In around 528 BC, he found the state of enlightenment (understanding) that he was seeking, and became known as Buddha (the enlightened one).

Wooden plaque showing the birth of Buddha, c.AD 100

Asoka

Asoka encouraged the spread of Buddhism in India by sending out missionaries and building shrines. He made laws to reduce poverty, which were carved on pillars topped by lions.

The beginning of Buddhism

Buddha dedicated the rest of his life to teaching his ideas to others. After his death, the faith gradually spread beyond India until it became widespread in many Far Eastern countries.

Buddhist carving, c.500 BC

Spread of Buddhism

Date	Place	Information
c.AD 50	China	Buddhism reached China during the Han dynasty. It was banned under the T'ang dynasty in 845.
c.550	Japan	Monks from Japan persuaded the Japanese emperor to adopt the faith, making it the country's official religion.
c.600	Tibet	Monks from India converted Tibetan nobles and kings, and the faith was gradually accepted over the next 200 years.

Ancient China

China was a series of independent states until the country was united under the Ch'in dynasty in 221 BC. This dynasty was short-lived and ended in a period of civil war, after which the strong Han dynasty took over, lasting for four centuries.

Paper mould

Paper and printing

The Chinese came up with many inventions long before they were thought of in the West. They guarded the secret of paper-making for 700 years, and also invented a system of printing using woodblocks.

The Great Wall

The first Chinese Emperor, Ch'in Shih huang-ti, joined together existing fortifications to create the 3,000-km (1,864-mile) Great Wall. It provided defence against raiding barbarians from the north. At first, the Great Wall was simply an earth rampart with a wooden fence.

2000 BC | 1000 BC | **250 BC** | 0 | **AD 200** | AD 600

CH'IN DYNASTY

- This dynasty lasted from 221 BC to 206 BC.
- They introduced standard weights and measures.
- They kept invaders from the north and south at bay.

HAN DYNASTY

- This dynasty lasted from 202 BC to AD 220.
- They showed more concern for the well-being of the peasants.
- They opened the silk routes to develop trade with the West.

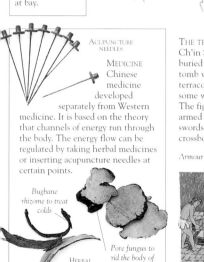

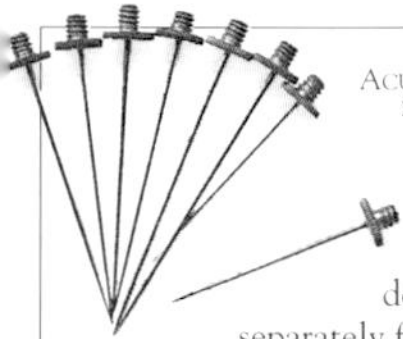

ACUPUNCTURE NEEDLES

MEDICINE

Chinese medicine developed separately from Western medicine. It is based on the theory that channels of energy run through the body. The energy flow can be regulated by taking herbal medicines or inserting acupuncture needles at certain points.

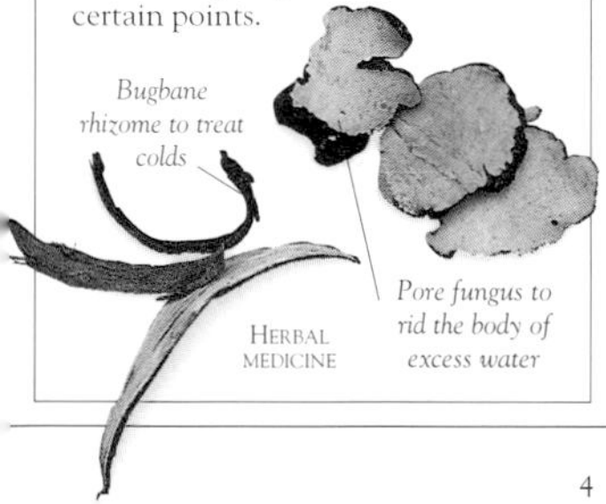

Bugbane rhizome to treat colds

Pore fungus to rid the body of excess water

HERBAL MEDICINE

THE TERRACOTTA ARMY

Ch'in Shih huang-ti was buried in an enormous tomb with 7,000 terracotta soldiers, some with horses. The figures are armed with real swords and crossbows.

Armour

THE ROMANS

FROM ITS BEGINNINGS as a shepherd's village in central Italy, Rome grew into the centre of a vast empire. After a period of civil wars, starting in in 49 BC, Octavian (63 BC–AD 14) defeated his rival Mark Antony (82 BC–30 BC) and became the first Roman emperor.

AUGUSTUS
When Julius Caesar's adopted son Octavian became Emperor in 27 BC, he changed his name to Augustus, which means revered.

ITALY
Rome
Mediterranean Sea

REPUBLIC IN 200 BC
REPUBLIC IN 133 BC
EMPIRE IN AD 1

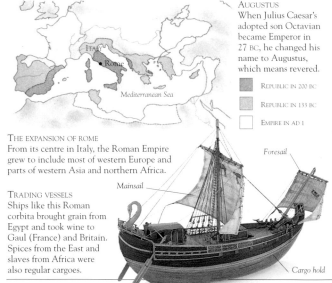

THE EXPANSION OF ROME
From its centre in Italy, the Roman Empire grew to include most of western Europe and parts of western Asia and northern Africa.

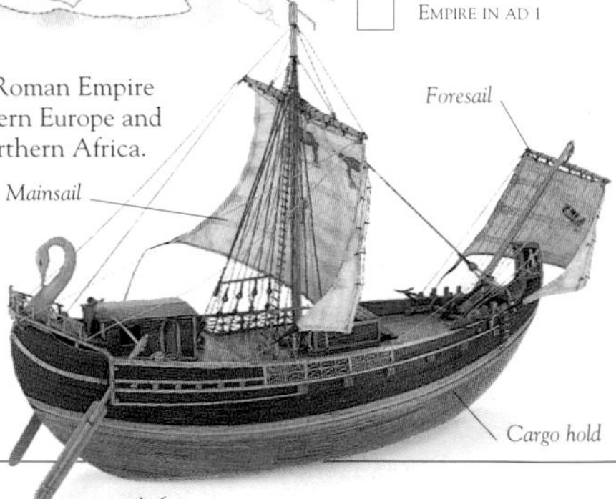

Mainsail
Foresail
Cargo hold

TRADING VESSELS
Ships like this Roman corbita brought grain from Egypt and took wine to Gaul (France) and Britain. Spices from the East and slaves from Africa were also regular cargoes.

Famous Romans

- Julius Caesar (100 BC–44 BC) became Dictator of Rome in 46 BC.
- Emperor Trajan (AD 53–117) extended the empire eastwards.
- Emperor Diocletian (245–313) brought order to the empire after a period of disruption.

The Roman army

Soldier

A vital force

The Roman army won conquests all over the Mediterranean, in Gaul, and in Britain. The army was also responsible for building the roads that criss-crossed the empire.

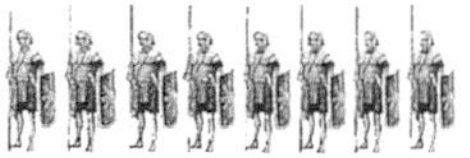
Contubernium

Organization

The army was made up of legions of 5,000 men. Each legion was divided into centuries (80 men), split into contubernia (eight men).

Century

Pont du Gard

The Romans built many aqueducts to provide their cities with water supplies.

Roman technology

Concrete was a very useful Roman invention. Instead of having to use stone or bricks, Roman builders could set concrete in all sorts of shapes, including domes and arches.

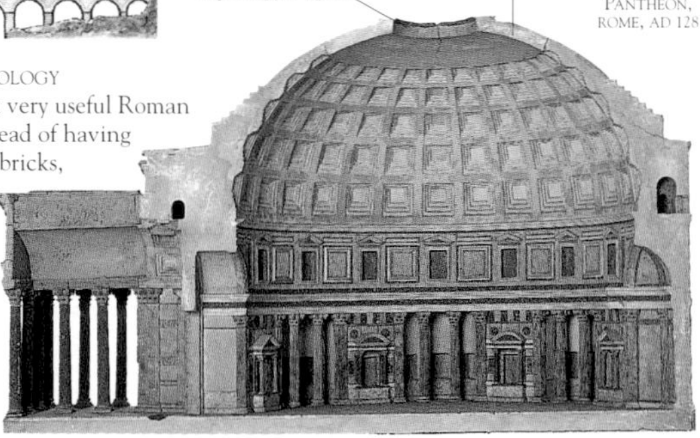

Oculus (opening for light)

Concrete dome

Pantheon, Rome, AD 128

The Rise of Christianity

CHRISTIANITY BEGAN as a minority sect in the eastern Mediterranean. Missionaries eventually spread the faith to Rome, but Christians were persecuted there until the fourth century, when the faith was accepted by the Emperor Constantine.

The Fall of Rome

The Roman Empire began to decline in the third century.

- The empire was too big to be controlled from one centre.
- The emperors relied on army support in order to rule.
- Local barbarian rulers became increasingly powerful.

The Spread of Christianity

In the early fourth century, the king of Axum, a trading empire in northeast Africa, converted to Christianity. By the fifth century, the faith was widespread in Axum.

AXUM OBELISK c.350

EARLY CHRISTIAN FISH SYMBOL

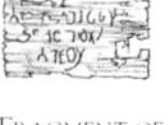

FRAGMENT OF GOSPEL TEXT

The Birth of Christianity

Christianity is based on the life and teachings of Jesus Christ (c.4 BC–AD 30), which are recorded in the four gospels in the New Testament. The Roman and Jewish authorities crucified Jesus because they thought that he was a revolutionary.

EMPEROR CONSTANTINE

People Who Helped to Spread Christianity

Name	Dates	Information
St Paul	c.AD 3–68	Christian missionary who spread the faith through Arabia, Syria, Greece, and Rome.
Emperor Constantine	280–337	Gave Christians in Rome the freedom to worship.
Emperor Theodosius I	347–395	Made Christianity the official religion of the Roman Empire.

The Byzantine Empire

After the fall of Rome, the eastern capital of the Roman Empire, Byzantium, was renamed Constantinople and became the centre of a new Christian empire that lasted until 1453. The core of the Byzantine Empire was modern Turkey and Greece.

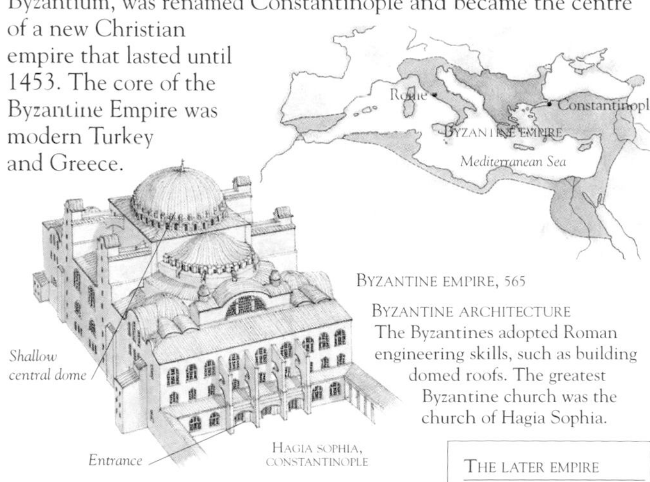

BYZANTINE EMPIRE, 565

HAGIA SOPHIA, CONSTANTINOPLE

BYZANTINE ARCHITECTURE

The Byzantines adopted Roman engineering skills, such as building domed roofs. The greatest Byzantine church was the church of Hagia Sophia.

BYZANTINE ART

The craft-workers of Byzantium were famous for their metalwork, jewellery, and carvings in wood and ivory. This hunting horn is delicately carved from a single elephant tusk.

Carved animals and birds

BYZANTINE HUNTING HORN

THE LATER EMPIRE

- Justinian I (483–565) reformed laws and brought North Africa and Spain under Byzantine rule.
- In 1204, Crusaders sacked Constantinople.
- Constantinople was taken over by Ottoman Turks in 1453, ending the empire.

American civilizations

THE AMERICAS WERE HOME to a host of different civilizations. Although they all had distinctive and sophisticated cultures with complex religious and social systems, none of these peoples developed metal-working skills. They used copper, gold, and silver, but mainly for making decorative items. Their tools were made from stone or obsidian (volcanic glass).

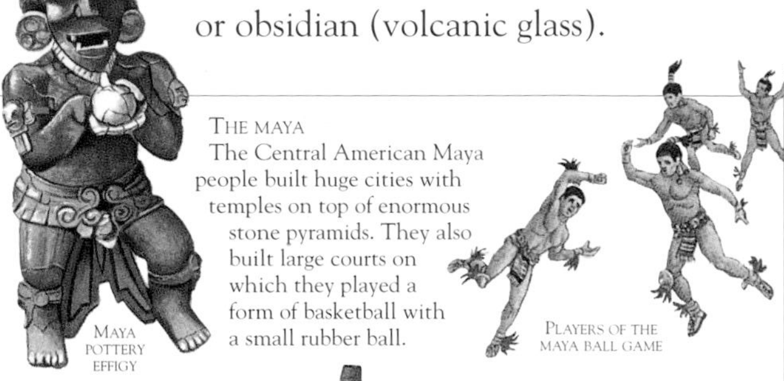

MAYA POTTERY EFFIGY

THE MAYA

The Central American Maya people built huge cities with temples on top of enormous stone pyramids. They also built large courts on which they played a form of basketball with a small rubber ball.

PLAYERS OF THE MAYA BALL GAME

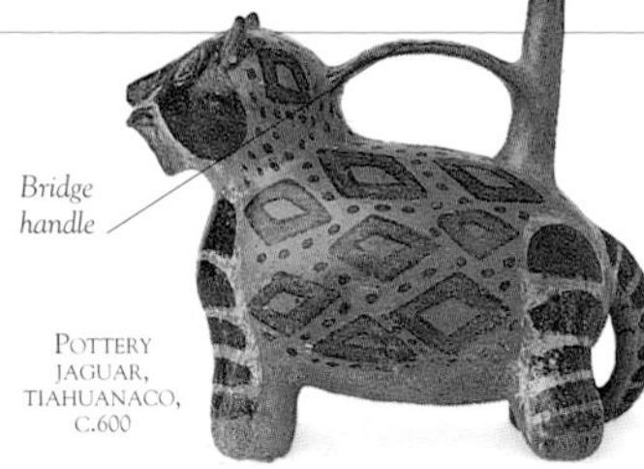

POTTERY JAGUAR, TIAHUANACO, C.600

TIAHUANACO

The centre of the empire of Tiahuanaco was near Lake Titicaca in Bolivia. Together with the Huari people, its rulers controlled the whole Andean region of South America. Tiahuanaco was a religious centre, with many large stone ceremonial buildings.

When and where

Name	Date (height)	Location	Information
Maya	300–900	Peninsula in Mexico and Guatemala	Highly developed culture based in city-states; used stone tools; built pyramids and conducted elaborate religious rituals.
Tiahuanaco	500–1000	Lake Titicaca in Bolivia	Built cities with stone temple enclosures; made mask-like sandstone sculptures and pottery images of gods.
Teotihuacan	100 BC–AD 750	Mexico	City-state on the central Mexican plateau laid out in a grid plan around a temple.
Hopewell	100 BC–AD 600	Mississippi and Ohio River Valleys	Mound-building culture of southern North America.

Teotihuacan

This was one of the most successful cities of central Mexico. The huge site, home to 100,000 people, contained 600 pyramids, 2,000 apartment blocks, and numerous workshops and squares. The people traded with their neighbours, the Maya.

Jaguar symbolizes fertility of soil

Jaguar god, Teotihuacan

Hopewell

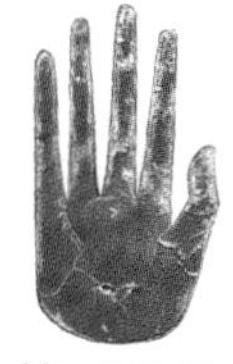

Mica hand from Hopewell mound

The North American Hopewell culture has become famous for its large burial mounds. Important Hopewell people were buried in these mounds with lavish grave goods brought from many places in North America.

Copper bird from Hopewell mound

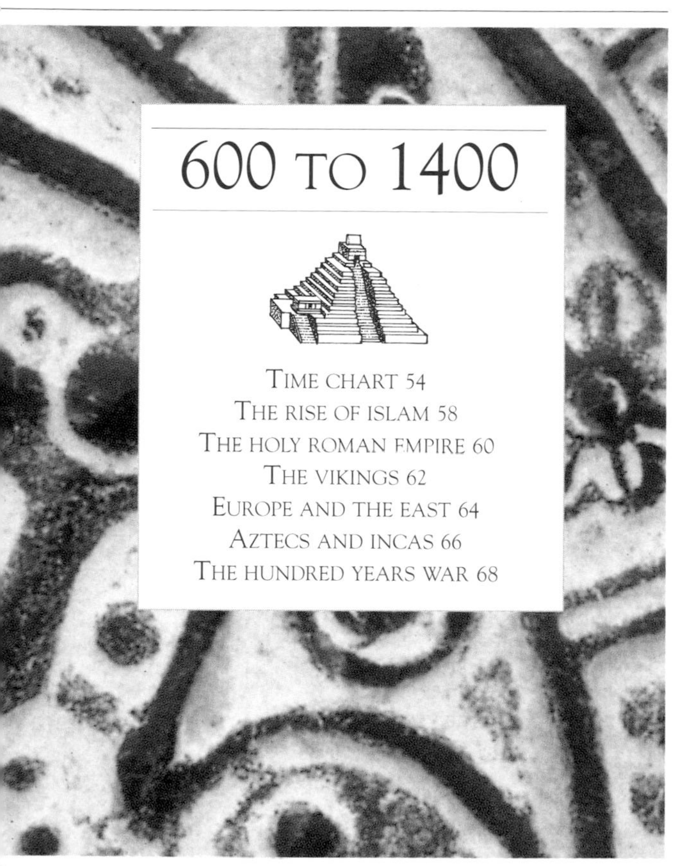

600 TO 1400

Time Chart

	600	675	750
EVENTS	**600** Height of Maya civilization, Central America ➡50 **610** Islamic religion founded ➡58 **618** China reunited by T'ang dynasty **622** Year one of Islamic calendar **637** Muslims conquer Jerusalem **642** Islam becomes major religion in Persia **647** Central Asian Hun tribes invade India, causing decline of Gupta Empire	**700** Franks develop feudal system ➡60 **c.700** Bantu Africans cross River Limpopo, taking iron-working technology south **c.700** Kingdom of Ghana prospers, West Africa **711** Moors (Muslims) invade Spain ➡58 **732** Moors defeated at Tours by Frankish leader Charles Martel (c.688–741), halting Islam's advance in Europe	**751** Muslims defeat Mongols at Samarkand **786** Harun-al-Rashid (766–809) becomes Caliph of Baghdad ➡59 **794** Kyoto, ancient capital of Japan, is established **800** Charlemagne (742–814) is crowned first Holy Roman Emperor ➡60 **c.800** Polynesian people (Maoris) reach New Zealand BANTU IRONWORKERS, C.700
ARTS & ARCHITECTURE	**618** Golden age of art and literature begins in China **650** Byzantine art and jewellery reaches its peak ➡49 BYZANTINE CROSS, 650	**689** Building starts on Dome of the Rock, Jerusalem **700s** Anglo–Saxon epic *Beowulf* written **745** First newspaper printed, China	**785** Building starts on Great Mosque at Córdoba, Spain **792** Building starts on Charlemagne's palace, Aix-la-Chapelle (Aachen), France **c.800** *Book of Kells* produced, Ireland
SCIENCE & INVENTION	**618** Paper money used, China **635** Quill pen first used for writing, Spain **650** Windmill first used, Persia ➡59	**700** Porcelain drinking vessels used, China **740** Printing with carved wood blocks developed in Japan and China; it is first used for printing prayers	**751** Arabs learn craft of paper-making from Chinese prisoners ➡59 **800s** Viking ships are the fastest ships of their time ➡62 **820** Algebra invented, Persian Empire

825	900	975
VIKING SHIPS, 800s **844** Kenneth McAlpine (d.858) defeats the Picts and unites Scotland **c.861** Vikings discover Iceland ➡ 63 **888** Chola dynasty of Tamil kings replaces Pallavas in southern India and Sri Lanka	**900** Hausa Kingdom of Daura founded, northern Nigeria **911** Viking leader Rollo (c.860–932) is granted Normandy ➡ 63 **920** Ghana's golden age begins **930** Córdoba becomes seat of Arab learning in Spain **950** Polynesian navigator Kupe arrives in New Zealand **960** Sung dynasty takes over China **962** Otto I (912–73) is crowned Holy Roman Emperor ➡ 61	**980** Arab traders settle on East African coast **980** Toltecs set up capital at Tula, Mexico ➡ 67 **c.982** Erik the Red (c.950–c.1010) establishes Viking settlement in Greenland ➡ 63 **989** Russians adopt Orthodox Christianity **997** Stephen I (977–1038) becomes King of Hungary **1000** Chimu civilization founded, Peru ➡ 67 **c.1000** Viking Leif Erikson reaches the coast of North America ➡ 63
848 Great Mosque of Samarra built, Iraq **868** The *Diamond Sutra*, a book of Buddhist scripture is published – the world's oldest printed book	**900s** Cathedrals built in Romanesque style all over western Europe **900** Organs first installed in abbeys and cathedrals, Europe **910** Benedictine abbey built, Cluny, France	**1000–1100** Temple of the Warriors built, Chichén Itzá, Mexico **1001** *Tale of Genji*, the first novel, is written by Japanese noblewoman, Murasaki Shikibu (978–c.1031) **1025** Music first written down as musical notation
850 Coffee discovered, East Africa **860** Cyrillic alphabet first used, eastern Europe CHINESE TYPESETTING, 995	**900s** Islamic medicine flourishes, Persia ➡ 59	**995** The Chinese experiment with reusable, movable type **1000** Spinning wheel appears, Asia **1044** Gunpowder invented, China; it is originally used for fireworks

TIME CHART

	1050	1125	1200
EVENTS	**1050** Almoravids (Berber Muslims) begin conquests of Morocco and parts of Spain **1066** William of Normandy (1027–87) defeats English King Harold (c.1020–66) at Battle of Hastings, and takes English throne ➡ 63 **1096** First Crusade begins ➡ 64 **1100** First Iron-Age settlement, Zimbabwe **1104** Crusaders capture Acre, Israel **1119** Bologna University founded, Italy	**1151** Fall of Toltec Empire, Mexico **1155** Paris University founded, France **1156** Civil war by rival clans in Japan leads to domination by samurai warlords **1167** Oxford University founded, England **1169** Saladin (1137–93) becomes ruler of Egypt **1187** Saladin captures Jerusalem from Crusaders **1191** Zen Buddhism introduced to Japan	**c.1200** Cuzco, Peru, becomes an Inca centre **1204** Fourth Crusaders sack Constantinople ➡ 64 **1206** Genghis Khan (1162–1227) founds Mongol Empire ➡ 65 **1215** John (1167–1216), King of England, seals Magna Carta **1235** Sun Diata (d.1255) founds Mali Empire, West Africa SAMURAI WARRIOR, 1156
ARTS & ARCHITECTURE	**1065** First known stained-glass windows, Augsberg, Germany **1066** Bayeux Tapestry made, France **1115** Philosopher Peter Abelard (1079–1142) begins teaching in Paris	**1132–44** St Denis Abbey built, France; first complete Gothic church **1174–75** Work begins on Old London Bridge, Avignon Bridge, and Pisa's Leaning Tower	**1200s** Christian churches built, Ethiopia **1200s** Gothic cathedrals built, western Europe **1200s** Great Buddha of Kamakura constructed, Japan **1200s** Many castles built, northern Europe
SCIENCE & INVENTION	**1050** Chinese use gunpowder for warfare **1090** Magnetic compass used, China and Arabia	**1180** Rudder used, Arabia **1190** Saracens use ships with stern rudders CHINESE USE GUNPOWDER, 1050	**1200** Magnifying glass invented, England **1200** Windmills used in Europe; the idea may have been brought from Asia by Crusaders **1232** Explosive rockets first used in war between Chinese and Mongols

1250	1300	1350
1250 Mamelukes (rebel slave soldiers) become rulers of Egypt **1250** Mayans restore empire and build new capital at Mayapan, Mexico **1271** Marco Polo (1254–1324) sets off from Venice for China **1273** Rudolf Habsburg (1218–91) becomes ruler of Germany, founding the powerful Habsburg dynasty ➡ 61 **1281** Mongol invaders driven from Japan **1291** Saracens capture Acre, ending Crusades	**1300** Incas begin major expansion through Andes ➡ 66 **1324** Mansa Musa (d.1332), Emperor of Mali, makes pilgrimage to Mecca **1325** Aztecs found Tenochtitlán, Mexico ➡ 66 **1337** Hundred Years War between England and France begins ➡ 68, 69 **1347** Black Death reaches Europe ➡ 69	**1352** Moroccan scholar Ibn Battuta (1304–68) travels across Sahara to Mali **1358** Jacquerie Revolt: French peasants revolt against raised taxes **1368** Tai Tsu (1328–98) founder of Ming dynasty, drives Mongols from China **1381** Peasants' Revolt, England **1398** Mongol leader Tamerlane (1336–1405) sacks Delhi, India
1250 Lute first brought to Europe from Islamic world	**1300s** Statues erected on Easter Island **1300** Giotto (1266–1337) pioneers naturalism in painting	**1350** Maoris create rock art, New Zealand **1353** Giovanni Boccaccio (1313–75) writes *The Decameron* **1385** Geoffrey Chaucer (1345–1400) begins to write *The Canterbury Tales*
1250 Longbow invented, Wales ➡ 68 **1250** Tinplate first used for armour, Bohemia **1280** Mechanical clock invented, Europe **1290** Spectacles invented, Italy	**1300** Gunpowder first used in cannons, Europe **1300** Windmills first used to drain land, Netherlands **1320** Lace invented, France and Flanders **1326** Hand-gun firing bullets first used, Italy	**1350** Hand cannon invented, Europe **1350** Mechanical alarm clock invented, Germany **1373** Lock gates first used on Dutch canals to control navigation and drainage

MANSA MUSA

EASTER ISLAND STATUES, 1300s

THE RISE OF ISLAM

THE ISLAMIC RELIGION was founded in 610 when the prophet Muhammad (c.570–632) announced that a new faith had been revealed to him. By 750, Muslims (the followers of Islam) had conquered a huge Arab Empire, stretching from Persia across North Africa to Spain.

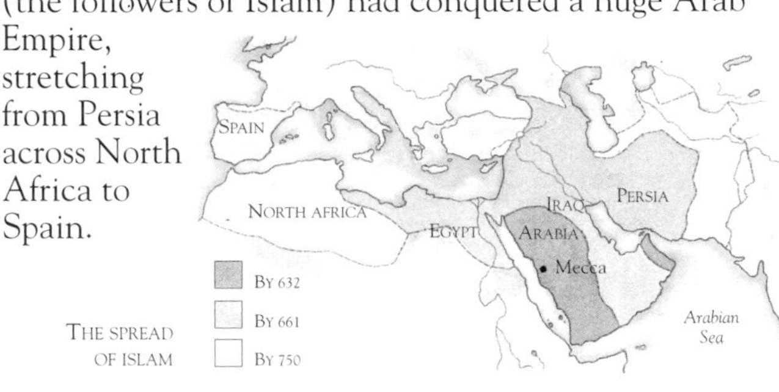

THE SPREAD OF ISLAM

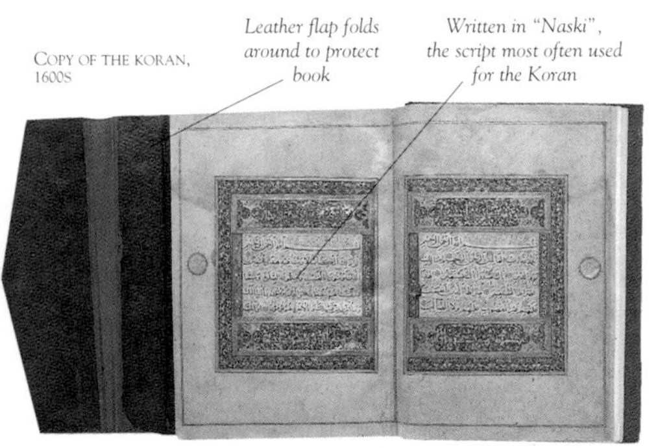

COPY OF THE KORAN, 1600S

Leather flap folds around to protect book

Written in "Naski", the script most often used for the Koran

THE ISLAMIC FAITH
The central beliefs of Islam are recorded in the Koran (the Muslim sacred book). Muslims believe that there is only one God and that Muhammad is his prophet. They pray five times a day while facing the holy city of Mecca, and they fast during the month of Ramadan.

HARUN-AL-RASHID
Harun-al-Rashid (766–809) was Caliph (ruler) of the Islamic Empire at the height of its power. His court at Baghdad was a centre of wealth, business, and culture.

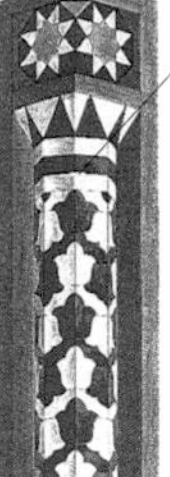

PESTLE AND MORTAR FOR MIXING MEDICINES

ISLAMIC ARCHITECTURE
The Islamic world developed its own style of architecture. The most typical buildings were mosques with domes and minarets (towers). Inside, a mihrab (niche) showed the direction of Mecca.

ISLAMIC MEDICINE
Islamic doctors treated medicine as a science. They performed minor operations, observed patients carefully, and used many different drugs.

ISLAMIC TECHNOLOGY

DEVELOPMENT		INFORMATION
Windmill, 650s		Windmills worked well on the windswept hills and plains of Persia. Islamic windmills had horizontal sails, but when Muslim colonists took the idea to Spain in the 10th century, they built mills with upright sails.
Lens, 1000s		The Islamic scholar Alhazen (c.965–1039) wrote the earliest reliable description of human vision. He was the first to use the term "lens", although glass lenses were probably not made until 200 years later.
Paper, 751		Paper was invented in China. Some Chinese paper-makers were captured by Muslims invading Samarkand in 751, and the craft of paper-making soon spread around the Islamic Empire.

THE HOLY ROMAN EMPIRE

ON CHRISTMAS DAY 800, the Frankish King Charles I (742–814) was crowned Holy Roman Emperor by the Pope. He was the first ruler to use this title, which was supposed to give him religious authority as well as the power of a great ruler. The core of the empire was modern-day Germany, parts of France, and northern Italy.

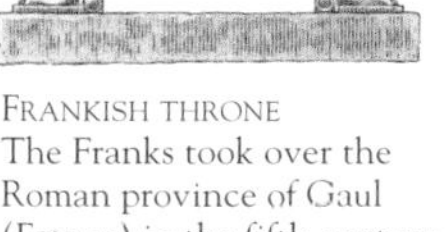

FRANKISH THRONE
The Franks took over the Roman province of Gaul (France) in the fifth century.

FEUDAL SYSTEM

The Franks devised the feudal system to run their empire.

- The emperor owned all the land.
- Nobles held land in return for providing services to the emperor.
- Tenants were given use of land in return for services to the nobles.

CHARLEMAGNE
Charles I was known as Charlemagne. He conquered most of western Europe, reformed the legal system, founded schools, and encouraged trade, agriculture, and the arts. His empire broke up some 30 years after his death.

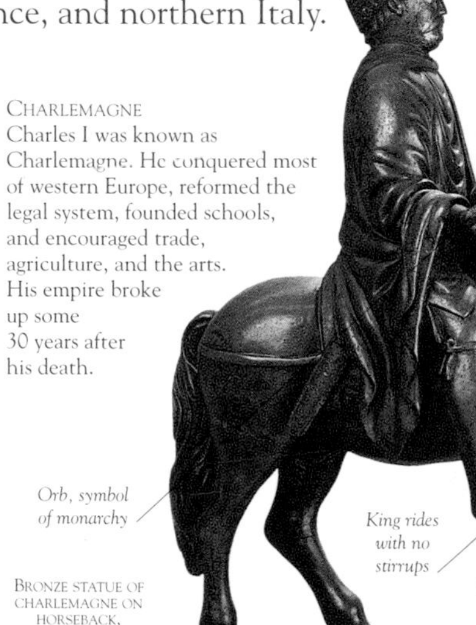

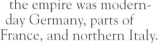

Orb, symbol of monarchy

King rides with no stirrups

BRONZE STATUE OF CHARLEMAGNE ON HORSEBACK, 800S

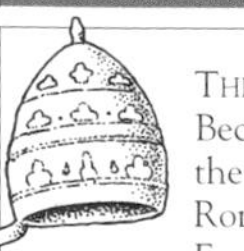

THE PAPACY
Because the Holy Roman Emperors claimed power over religious matters and the popes wielded great political power, the empire and the papacy were often in conflict over control of Europe.

GREAT MEDIEVAL EMPERORS

NAME	LIFE DATES	INFORMATION
Otto I	912–973	Revived the empire and defended it against the invading armies of the Magyars.
Frederick I	1123–1190	Attempted to settle internal conflicts in the Holy Roman Empire.
Frederick II	1194–1250	Crusading emperor who secured Jerusalem without fighting, but quarrelled with the Pope.
Rudolf	1218–1291	Duke of Austria who was the first emperor of the Habsburg dynasty.

IMPERIAL CROWN
After Charlemagne, there was no Holy Roman Emperor until Otto I was crowned in 962. The Holy Roman Empire lasted until 1806, when it was dissolved by Napoleon.

HOLY ROMAN EMPIRE, 987

THE HABSBURGS
The Habsburg family dominated Europe for centuries.

- From 1438 to 1806, every Holy Roman Emperor but one was a Habsburg.
- Habsburg power reached its peak with Emperor Charles V (1500–58), who was also King of Spain.

The Vikings

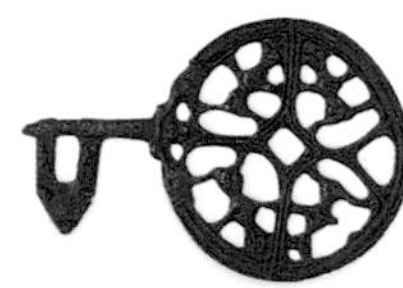

BRONZE KEY
A high-ranking Viking would keep his most precious possessions in a strong chest locked with an ornate key.

THE VIKINGS SET SAIL from their homelands in Norway, Sweden, and Denmark, raiding the coasts of Europe, plundering the lands, and often settling there. But not all Vikings were raiders. Some traded peacefully, selling goods such as furs, walrus tusks, whale oil, and timber.

TRADE AND INVASION
Viking merchants sailed around the Mediterranean and along the Dnieper and Volga Rivers. A shortage of farming land at home also led Vikings to set up colonies in Iceland, England, Ireland, and France.

LONGSHIPS
Viking warships had a single square sail, but could also be rowed. They were the fastest ships of their day.

ANIMAL HEAD
Viking chiefs were sometimes buried in their ships. This animal head was found in a buried Viking ship.

ᚠᚢᚦᚬᚱᚴᚼᚾᛁᛅᛋᛏᛒᛘᛚᛦ

F U TH A R K H N I A S T B M L R

VIKING RUNES

The Viking alphabet was known as the "futhark", after the first six runes (letters).

THOR'S HAMMER LUCKY CHARM, 1100S

VIKING COSTUME

In their cold homelands, Vikings wore warm woollen garments fastened with metal clasps and brooches. Fur trimmings provided extra warmth.

Leather purse

Gold brooch

RELIGION

The many Viking gods included Odin, the god of war, Frigg, the goddess of childbirth, and Thor, the god of thunder. According to legend, Thor's main weapon was his magic hammer.

EXPLORERS

- In c.861, Ingolf was the first Viking to reach Iceland.
- In c.982, Erik the Red (c.950–c.1010) reached Greenland and founded settlements.
- Erik's son Leif reached North America in c.1000. He called the new land Vinland (wineland).

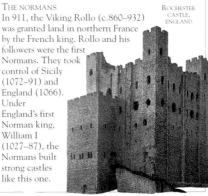

THE NORMANS

In 911, the Viking Rollo (c.860–932) was granted land in northern France by the French king. Rollo and his followers were the first Normans. They took control of Sicily (1072–91) and England (1066). Under England's first Norman king, William I (1027–87), the Normans built strong castles like this one.

ROCHESTER CASTLE, ENGLAND

Europe and the East

DURING THE 12TH AND 13TH centuries, religious tensions between Europeans and the Turks of western Asia led to the Crusades. Meanwhile, Europe's eastern borders were threatened by the powerful Mongol Empire.

MILITARY ORDERS
These are the shields of the Hospitallers and the Teutonic Knights, orders of fighting monks.

The Crusades

In 1095, Pope Urban II (c.1042–99) preached a sermon in which he encouraged Western leaders to recapture the holy lands of western Asia from the Muslim Turks. The result was a series of religious wars known as the Crusades.

MAJOR CRUSADES

Crusade	Date	Outcome
First Crusade	1096–1099	Crusaders take Antioch, then Jerusalem in July 1099.
Second Crusade	1147–1149	Poor leadership results in Crusaders' defeat in Anatolia.
Third Crusade	1189–1192	Crusaders take control of eastern Mediterranean coast.
Fourth Crusade	1202–1204	Crusaders plunder Constantinople; they do not reach the Holy Land.

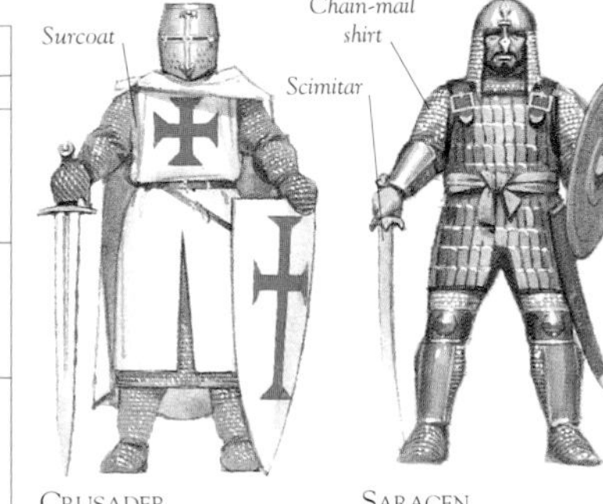

CRUSADER
The cross on the crusader's surcoat and shield showed that he was fighting for God.

SARACEN
Muslim warriors (Saracens) carried a round shield and a curved scimitar.

The Mongol Empire

At the end of the 12th century, a number of tribes from central Asia joined up under the leader Temujin (1162–1227) to form a Mongol army. They fought their way eastwards, quickly amassing a huge empire. Temujin was renamed Genghis Khan, (Absolute Ruler).

MONGOL LANDS

EMPIRE OF GENGHIS KHAN, C.1227

EMPIRE OF KUBLAI KHAN, C.1294

LANDS OF BOTH GENGHIS AND KUBLAI

MONGOL CAVALRYMEN

MONGOL WARRIORS
The key to the Mongols' military success was their cavalry. Mongol horsemen could fire arrows while riding at full speed. They could also travel fast – up to 120 km (75 miles) a day.

ARROWS
Mongol soldiers used arrows with whistling heads to signal during battle.

CHINESE SILK

TRADE WITH THE WEST
The Mongols controlled trade with the West by policing the Silk Road, a network of trade routes across Asia. Merchants exported silk, porcelain, lacquered goods, spices, and tea.

AZTECS AND INCAS

THE AZTECS WERE fierce warriors who settled in Mexico in the 13th century. The Incas were another warrior tribe who came to power further south, in the Andes. By the 15th century, these two empires dominated Central and South America.

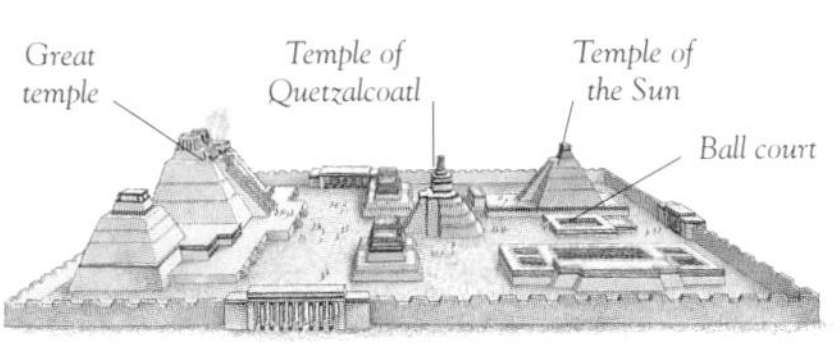

TENOCHTITLÁN
The Aztec capital, Tenochtitlán, was built on swampy land in Lake Texcoco. Three causeways linked it to the shore of the lake.

AZTEC AND INCA EMPIRES
The Aztecs ruled a compact empire in central Mexico. The Incas built a network of roads to improve communications in their large empire.

AZTEC SUN STONE
The Aztecs believed that the world had passed through four previous phases, and that the Sun, the Moon, and humanity were created in the fifth phase. This stone shows the Sun, the four previous phases of creation, and the 20 days of the Aztec month.

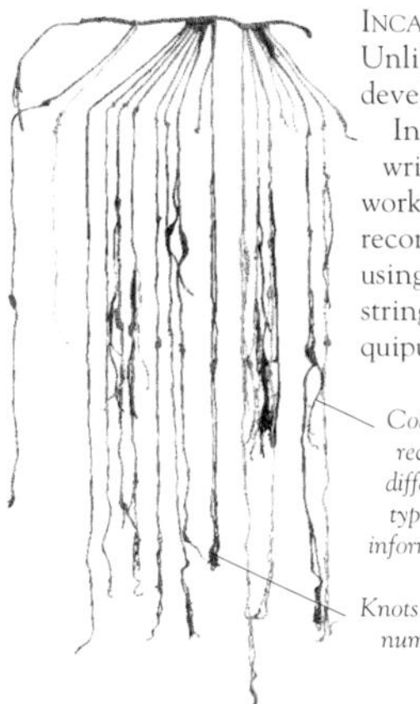
Colours record different types of information
Knots record numbers

INCA QUIPU

Unlike most other highly developed civilizations, the Incas had no system of writing. Instead, they worked out a way of recording information using knotted lengths of string called quipus.

RISE AND FALL

- The Aztec Empire reached its height in the 1420s. It fell to Spanish invaders (conquistadors) in 1520.
- The Incas grew in power in the early 1400s. Their empire was destroyed by the Spanish in 1532.

CEREMONIAL KNIFE

Knives like this were used to perform human sacrifices, which were an important part of Inca religion.

OTHER AMERICAN PEOPLES

THE TOLTECS

Before the Aztecs came to power, the Toltecs dominated many Mexican cities. Their capital was at Tula. Like the Aztecs and the Maya, the Toltecs farmed maize, built pyramid temples, and performed human sacrifices.

Priest

TOLTEC SACRIFICE

King is carried to his burial place in sitting position

CHIMU BURIAL CEREMONY

THE CHIMU

The Chimu ruled northern Peru until the 15th century. They built a network of roads leading to their capital, Chan Chan.

THE HUNDRED YEARS WAR

WHEN EDWARD III (1312–77) was crowned King of England in 1327, he thought he also had a good claim to the French throne through his mother. In 1337, he declared war on France, beginning a conflict that was to last over a hundred years, until the final French victory in 1453.

LONGBOWS
Longbows fired armour-piercing arrows and were quicker to load than crossbows.

THE SIEGE OF ORLÉANS
A turning point in the war came with the siege of this city in 1429. The English cut the city off for seven months, but French leader Joan of Arc attacked the English and broke the siege.

English troops guard approaches to city
French troops mount an attack

CHAIN MAIL
In the 14th century, soldiers wore shirts made of linked iron rings.

LEADERS OF THE HUNDRED YEARS WAR		
NAME	LIFE DATES	INFORMATION
Edward, the Black Prince	1330–1376	Son of Edward III who fought at the Battle of Crécy (1346) and captured the French king at Poitiers (1356).
Henry V	1387–1422	English king who defeated the French at Agincourt (1415) and was made heir to the French throne.
Joan of Arc	1412–1431	Inspirational French leader who was eventually burned at the stake at Rouen, charged with heresy.

PHASES OF THE WAR

- From 1337 to 1360, the English won much French territory.
- From 1364 to 1380, the French under Charles V (1337–80) began to reconquer lost lands.
- From 1420 to 1452, the French regained all their lost territory, except Calais.

The Black Death

In 1347, an epidemic swept across Europe. In four years, some 25 million people (about a quarter of the population) died of the Black Death, a combination of pneumonic and bubonic plague.

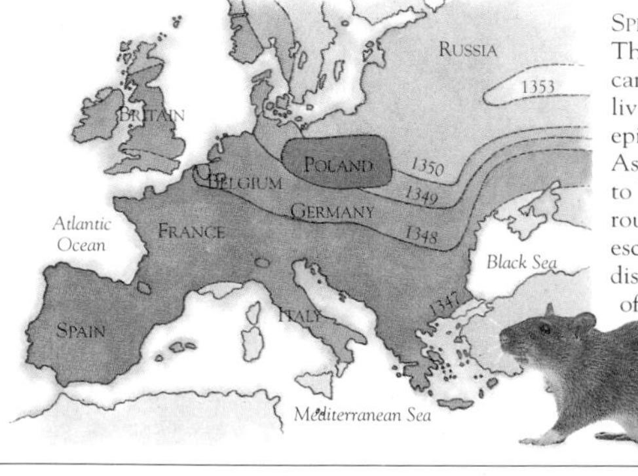

SPREAD OF THE PLAGUE
The Black Death was carried by fleas that lived on rats. The epidemic originated in Asia and rapidly spread to Europe along trade routes. Only a few areas escaped the dreadful disease, including parts of Poland, Flanders, southwest France, and Milan.

1400 TO 1750

TIME CHART

	1400	1435	1470
EVENTS	**1400s** Expansion of Inca and Aztec Empires ➡ 66, 67 **1400s** Trading empires flourish, Africa ➡ 85 **1404** Chinese navigator Cheng Ho (1371–1435) sets off on his first voyage ➡ 79 **1405** Fall of Mongol Empire **1415** Battle of Agincourt: English defeat French ➡ 69 **1429** Joan of Arc (1412–31) leads French at Siege of Orléans ➡ 68, 69	**1450** Machu Picchu founded, Peru **1453** End of Hundred Years War ➡ 68, 69 **1453** Fall of Constantinople ends Byzantine Empire ➡ 49, 82 JOAN OF ARC **1455–85** Wars of the Roses, England; royal houses of Lancaster and York fight over rival claims to the throne **1464** Sonni Ali (d.1492) becomes ruler of Songhai, West Africa	**1479** Spain united under Ferdinand of Aragon (1452–1516) and Isabella of Castille (1451–1504) ➡ 78 **1480** Spanish Inquisition starts ➡ 78 **1485** Henry VII (1457–1509) becomes first Tudor King of England and Wales after Battle of Bosworth ends Wars of the Roses **1492** Italian explorer Christopher Columbus (1451–1506) reaches Americas
ARTS & ARCHITECTURE	**1400s** Oil painting becomes popular as patrons demand pictures such as portraits **1400s** Renaissance begins in Italy ➡ 76, 77	**1446** Dome of Florence Cathedral completed, Italy **c.1450** Building at Great Zimbabwe, Africa, at its height **1456** First printed Bible	MING BOWL, 1490s **1488** Ming emperor orders rebuilding of Great Wall of China **1490s** Chinese blue-and-white Ming porcelain exported to Europe
SCIENCE & INVENTION	GREAT ZIMBABWE, C.1450 **1405** Metal screw used, Germany **1410** Coil spring used in clocks, Italy	**1451** Printing with metal movable type invented; printing presses are rapidly set up all over Europe	**1470** Mariner's astrolabe invented, Europe **1495** Double entry book-keeping invented, Venice, Italy **1498** Toothbrush first used, China

1500	1535	1570
1517 Reformation begins, Europe ➡ 80, 81 **1519–32** Aztec and Inca empires destroyed ➡ 67, 86 **1520** Suleiman (1494–1566) becomes Ottoman emperor ➡ 82 **1522** After death of Ferdinand Magellan (1480–1521), his crew complete first round-the-world voyage **1534** Henry VIII (1491–1547) creates Church of England ➡ 81 **1534** St Ignatius Loyola (1491–1556) founds Jesuit order	**1542** Portuguese traders reach Japan **1553** Lady Jane Grey (1537–54) is Queen of England for nine days **1556** Akbar (1542–1605) becomes Mogul Emperor of India ➡ 83 **1556** Philip II (1527–98) becomes King of Spain ➡ 81 **1558** Elizabeth I (1533–1603) becomes Queen of England	**1571** Ottoman fleet defeated at Battle of Lepanto **1572** St Bartholomew's Day Massacre of Protestants, France ➡ 81 **1577–80** Francis Drake (c.1545–96) sails around the world **1588** English fleet defeats Spanish Armada ➡ 81 SPANISH ARMADA, 1588
1503 Leonardo da Vinci (1452–1519) begins to paint the *Mona Lisa* **1512** Michelangelo Buonarotti (1475–1564) completes Sistine Chapel frescoes, Italy	**1552** François Rabelais (c.1494–c.1553) completes *Gargantua and Pantagruel* **1555–60** St Basil's Cathedral built, Moscow **1559–84** Building of palace of Escorial, Madrid, Spain	**1590** El Greco (1541–1614) paints *St Jerome* **1590** William Shakespeare (1564–1616) begins to write plays **1594** First opera, *Dafne* by Jacopo Peri (1561–1633), produced
1509 Wallpaper first used, England **1511** Watch invented, Germany **1519** Chocolate first brought to Europe from Mexico **1530** Corks used to stop bottles, western Europe	**1543** Nicolas Copernicus (1473–1543) states that Earth and the other planets orbit the Sun **1569** Gerhard Kremer Mercator (1512–94) creates his new world map on a projection still used today	**1573** Potatoes first brought to Europe from Peru **1592** Galileo Galilei (1564–1642) invents the thermometer POTATO PLANT, 1573

	1600	1625	1650
EVENTS	**1600** Tokugawa period begins, Japan ➡84 **1600–14** English, Dutch, Danish, and French East India Companies founded ➡86, 87 **1603** James VI (1566–1625) of Scotland becomes James I of England **1618** Thirty Years War begins, Europe **1620** *Mayflower* sails to America  THE MAYFLOWER, 1620	**1626** Dutch found New Amsterdam (now New York) **1642** Explorer Abel Tasman (1603–59) reaches Tasmania and New Zealand **1642–49** English Civil War ➡88 **1643** Reign of Louis XIV (1638–1715) begins, France ➡88 **1644** Manchu dynasty founded, China ➡89 **1649** Charles I (b.1600) executed, England ➡88	**1653–58** Protectorate of Oliver Cromwell (1599–1658), England **1658** Reign of Aurangzeb (1618–1707), last great Mogul emperor, begins, India **1660** Charles II (1630–85) restored to English throne **1664** English seize New Amsterdam from Dutch and rename it New York **1665** Great Plague in London **1666** Great Fire of London
ARTS & ARCHITECTURE	**1603** Kabuki theatre begins, Japan **1605** First part of *Don Quixote* by Miguel Cervantes (1547–1616) published **1606** Building of Blue Mosque starts, Istanbul	**1632** Building of Taj Mahal begins, India **1636** High point of Flemish and Dutch art  TAJ MAHAL, 1632	**1656** Piazza of St Peter's built, Rome **1661** Building of Palace of Versailles begins, France ➡88
SCIENCE & INVENTION	**1619–28** William Harvey (1578–1657) investigates blood circulation **1623** First mechanical calculator invented, Germany **1624** Primitive submarine demonstrated in River Thames, London	**1632** Galileo supports the theory that the Earth and other planets orbit the Sun; in 1633, he is forced to retract his support by the Inquisition **1637** Umbrella made from oiled cloth used, France	**1650** Vacuum pump invented, Germany **1656** Pendulum clock invented, Netherlands **1661** First banknotes issued by Bank of Sweden **1667** First successful blood transfusion, France

1675	1700	1725
1675 War between colonists and Native Americans devastates New England **1677** Ottoman Empire at war with Russia **1680** Extinction of dodo **1682** Reign of Peter the Great (1672–1725) begins, Russia ➔89 **1689** William of Orange (1650–1702) becomes joint sovereign of Britain with his wife, Mary II (1662–94) **1690s** Asante kingdom established on Gold Coast, Africa ➔85	**1700s** Enlightenment begins, Europe ➔96, 97 **1701–13** Much of Europe is involved in War of Spanish Succession, which begins after death of Charles II of Spain (1665–1700) **1707** Act of Union joins England and Scotland **1715** Jacobites rise up and attempt to restore Stuart king to British throne **1721** Robert Walpole (1676–1745) becomes first British prime minister	**1727** Coffee first grown, Brazil **1737** Earthquake kills 300,000 people, India **1739** Spain and Britain fight for control of North American and Caribbean waters **1740** Frederick the Great (1712–86) becomes King of Prussia **1741** Vitus Bering (1681–1741) discovers strait between Russia and Alaska **1746** Battle of Culloden ends second Jacobite rising, Scotland

ST PETERSBURG, 1703

1675	1700	1725
1675 Rebuilding of St Paul's Cathedral, London begins, to a design by Christopher Wren (1632–1723) **1677** Jean Racine (1639–99) writes his tragedy *Phèdre*	**1703** St Petersburg founded, Russia **1709** Piano invented, Italy **1717** Georg Friederich Handel (1685–1759) writes his *Water Music*	**1726** *Gulliver's Travels* by Jonathan Swift (1667–1745) published **1729** Johann Sebastian Bach (1685–1750) writes his choral work *St Matthew Passion*
1675 Pocket watch invented, Netherlands **1675** Scientist and astronomer, Isaac Newton (1642–1727) experiments with static electricity ➔96	**1712** Steam engine invented, England **1714** Mercury thermometer invented, Germany	**1733** Mechanized weaving invented, England **1733** Natural rubber discovered in rainforests of Peru **1741** Centigrade scale first used on thermometers

ISAAC NEWTON

The Renaissance

In the 14th and 15th centuries, the Renaissance, a rebirth of interest in the culture of ancient Greece and Rome, began in northern Italy and spread throughout Europe. Scholars and artists were inspired by the rediscovery of Greek and Roman ideas about art, literature, and science.

Lorenzo de Medici medallion

Basilica of St Peter's, Rome, 1506–1626

Patrons

Rich, noble families such as the Medicis ruled Italian city-states. Many of them showed off their wealth and status by becoming patrons of the arts.

Classical style

Architects turned their back on the gothic style of the Middle Ages. New buildings followed the proportions of the buildings of ancient Greece and Rome. The exteriors were decorated with columns, and they were often roofed with domes.

Renaissance families

- The Medicis ruled Florence from 1434 to 1737. Their wealth came from banking.
- The Borgias were powerful in Rome in the 15th and 16th centuries. Two of the Borgias became popes.

1600 | 1700 | 1750

THE SCHOOL OF ATHENS, BY RAPHAEL, 1511

Statue is 5.49 m (18 ft) high

DAVID, BY MICHELANGELO, 1504

VISUAL ARTS

As well as traditional religious themes and portraits of their patrons, artists portrayed subjects from the history and mythology of the ancient world. All were painted and sculpted with a new realism.

SCIENCE AND TECHNOLOGY

- Printing with metal movable type was invented by German goldsmith Johannes Gutenberg (1400–68) in 1451.
- Italian artist and inventor Leonardo da Vinci (1452–1519) made designs for a helicopter, a parachute, and a flying machine with flapping wings.

PEOPLE OF THE RENAISSANCE

NAME	DATES	INFORMATION
Desiderius Erasmus	1466–1536	Dutch scholar, philosopher, and writer; translator of New Testament.
Niccolò Machiavelli	1469–1527	Italian statesman and writer of books on government.
Michelangelo Buonarotti	1475–1564	Italian painter, sculptor, architect, and poet.
Andreas Vesalius	1514–1564	Belgian writer of first accurate book on human anatomy.

Spain and Portugal

In the 15th century, Spain and Portugal were two of the most powerful countries in Europe. They both began to set up great world empires.

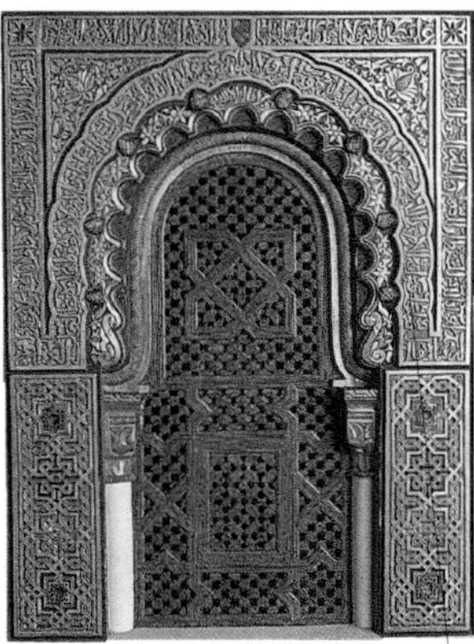

Arch, the Alhambra, 1334–54

Inscription

Reconquest of Spain

From the 11th century onwards, Christian leaders of various Spanish regions began to recapture parts of the country from its Islamic rulers. By 1248, most of Spain had been recovered.

Islamic Spain
The Muslims had constructed many fine buildings in Spain including the palace of the Alhambra in Granada.

Religious intolerance

- Ferdinand and Isabella set up the Spanish Inquisition to seek out heretics.
- Thousands of Jews were given the choice of becoming Christian or leaving Spain.

United Spain
In 1479, Spain was united after the marriage of Ferdinand of Aragon (1452–1516) and Isabella of Castille (1451–1504).

Exploration

In 1416, Portuguese Prince Henry the Navigator (1394–1460) founded a school of navigation and began to send out ships to explore the coast of Africa.

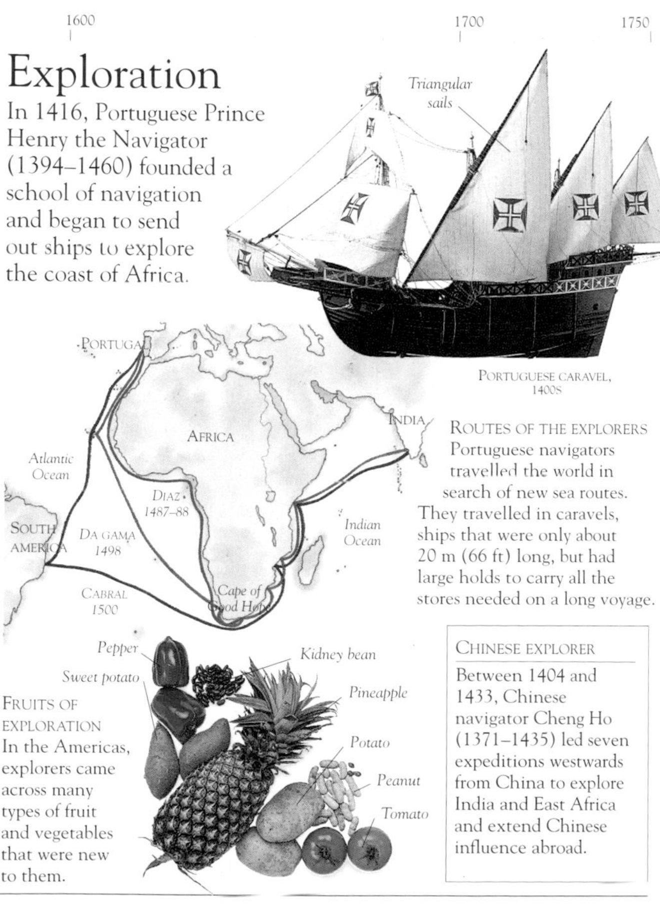

PORTUGUESE CARAVEL, 1400S

ROUTES OF THE EXPLORERS
Portuguese navigators travelled the world in search of new sea routes. They travelled in caravels, ships that were only about 20 m (66 ft) long, but had large holds to carry all the stores needed on a long voyage.

FRUITS OF EXPLORATION
In the Americas, explorers came across many types of fruit and vegetables that were new to them.

CHINESE EXPLORER
Between 1404 and 1433, Chinese navigator Cheng Ho (1371–1435) led seven expeditions westwards from China to explore India and East Africa and extend Chinese influence abroad.

The Reformation

Corruption within the Catholic Church during the 16th century sparked off a religious movement called the Reformation. Violent conflicts broke out between Catholics and the reformers, who were known as Protestants. All over Europe, new churches were set up.

Luther's 95 theses

Martin Luther

Martin Luther

German reformer Martin Luther (1483–1546) objected to the Catholic Church's sale of indulgences, which were promises of God's forgiveness in return for money. In 1517, Luther compiled a list of 95 theses (arguments) against indulgences and nailed it to the church door at Wittenberg.

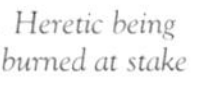

Heretic being burned at stake

Religious upheaval

People who wanted to worship in a different way or who attacked the power of the Catholic Church were often severely punished. Some were even burned alive.

Reformation aims

- Religious teachings should be based more closely on the words of the Bible.
- The Bible should be translated into major European languages.

PHILIP II OF SPAIN

THE SPANISH ARMADA

In 1588, Philip (1527–98) sent a fleet, the Spanish Armada, to invade England so that he could restore Catholic rule. The Armada was defeated, and England remained Protestant.

DAGGER OF HENRY IV OF FRANCE

THE FRENCH STRUGGLE

After years of religious conflict, Protestant King Henry IV (1553–1610) established religious toleration in France.

GERMAN PEASANTS' WAR

Encouraged by the teachings of Luther, German peasants rose up against their lords in 1524, demanding better conditions. They hoped for Luther's support, but he supported the lords. Within a year, the revolt was crushed.

Soldiers crush the revolt mercilessly

REFORMATION EVENTS

EVENT	DATE	INFORMATION
English break with Rome	1534	Henry VIII (1491–1547) wanted to divorce his first wife, but divorce was not permitted under Catholicism, so Henry took over the English Church himself.
Dutch rebellions	1568–1648	The Netherlands were part of the Spanish Empire, but the mainly Protestant Dutch wanted to be independent. After numerous rebellions, independence came in 1648.
St Bartholomew's Day Massacre, France	1572	In a clash between Huguenots (Protestants) and Catholics, thousands of Protestant men, women, and children were killed, both in Paris and the provinces.

New empires

Several large empires in Asia and Africa reached their height in the 16th century. The Ottoman and Mogul Empires were ruled by strong Muslim leaders who established efficient new systems of government.

Stylized patterns show Chinese influence

Ottoman Empire

Ottoman (Turkish) rulers considered it their duty to conquer other peoples and convert them to Islam. By the reign of Suleiman I (1494–1566), the empire was one of the most powerful ever known, and stretched across three continents: Asia, Europe, and Africa.

Art
The artistic styles of peoples within the expanding empire influenced Ottoman artists and craft-workers.

Extent of the empire
The Ottomans conquered the Byzantine city of Constantinople in 1453. They renamed it Istanbul, and made it the capital of their vast empire.

Suleiman I
A renowned military leader, Suleiman was known to his people as al-Qanuni or the Law-giver.

DAGGER
Worn just for show rather than as a weapon, this dagger is beautifully engraved with lines of poetry.

OTTOMAN GOVERNMENT

- Suleiman presided over a civil service staffed with highly trained officials.
- The top officials were slaves who had been trained for their government jobs from childhood.

Mogul Empire

In 1500, India was divided up into warring Hindu and Muslim states. Descendants of the Mongols, the Muslim Moguls swept down from the north and took over much of India, which they ruled until 1858.

Akbar discussing religious beliefs

AKBAR
Although Emperor Akbar (1542–1605) was a Muslim, he was tolerant of other religions, and allowed people to worship freely.

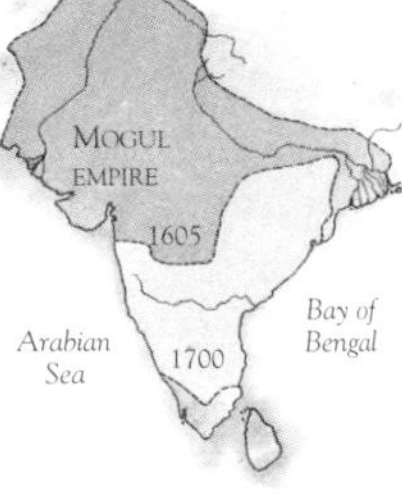

EXTENT OF THE EMPIRE
At its greatest extent in 1700, the Mogul Empire reached almost to the southern tip of India.

WEAPONRY
A samurai carried two swords and a dagger.

Tokugawa Japan

Japan's head of state was the emperor, but the most powerful person was actually the shogun, who ruled on his behalf. In the late 16th century, politician and general Tokugawa Ieyasu (1543–1616) defeated his rivals and became shogun. The Tokugawa family continued to rule Japan until 1867.

Armour

Bow

SAMURAI
The Samurai were trained warriors who served a lord and kept law and order.

JAPANESE CASTLE
The shogun ruled with the help of local lords called daimyo. The daimyo built castles from which they could control their local area.

Wooden upper storey

Narrow window openings

Wooden shingles

Plastered wall

Gun loop

FOREIGN RELATIONS
By 1650, Japan's only contact with the outside world was through Dutch and Chinese trading posts like this one.

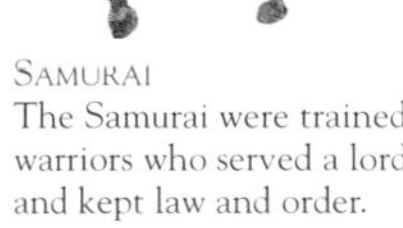

African empires

Religion and culture

- Many North African empires were mainly Muslim.
- Universities were set up at the trading centres of Jenne and Timbuktu in the Songhai Empire.
- African empires built large walled cities with mosques.

African states such as the Mali and Songhai Empires grew wealthy from trade in goods such as gold, copper, and salt. These empires were often held together by a combination of a strong ruler and an effective legal system.

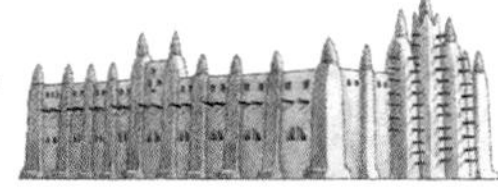

SONGHAI MOSQUE
This mud-brick mosque was first built in the 14th century.

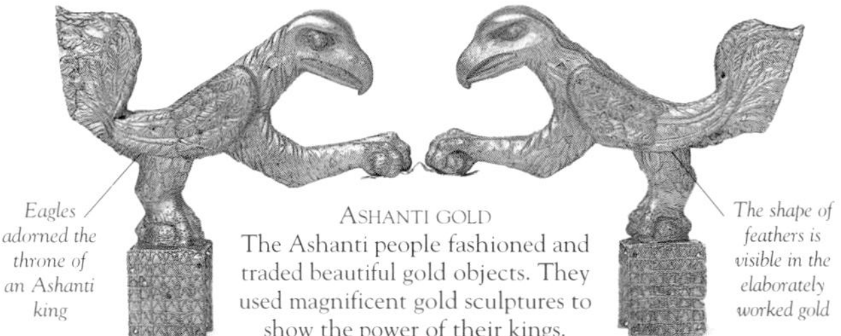

Eagles adorned the throne of an Ashanti king

ASHANTI GOLD
The Ashanti people fashioned and traded beautiful gold objects. They used magnificent gold sculptures to show the power of their kings.

The shape of feathers is visible in the elaborately worked gold

Great empires of Africa

Empire	Height	Information
Mali	1200–1400	Large, Muslim West African empire, with an efficient legal system and many trading links.
Benin	1200–1900	Kingdom in West Africa, famous for its superb craftsmanship in wood, stone, and bronze.
Songhai	1400–1600	Great Muslim trading empire that grew from its base in Mali to include large areas of West Africa.
Ashanti	1600–1900	West African state that set up an African coastal trading network.

ASHANTI SCULPTURE

COLONY AND TRADE

JOURNEYS OF explorers in the 15th and 16th centuries gave European traders new routes to the Far East and new trade destinations. Organizations such as the East India Companies of France, England, and the Netherlands set up trading stations in the Far East, which eventually became colonies. European settlers began to found colonies all over the world.

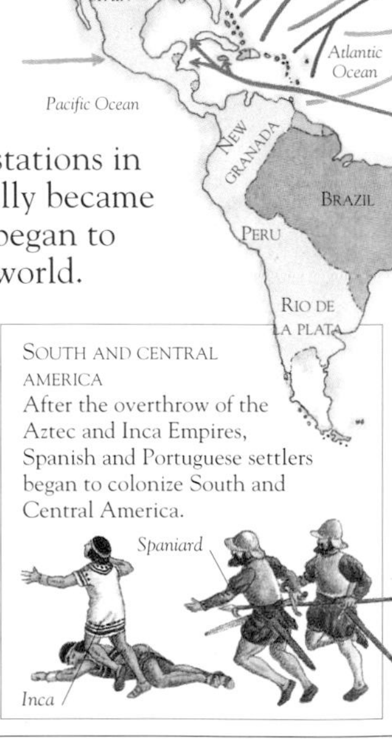

NORTH AMERICA

Europeans began to colonize North America from the late 15th century. Many settlers were escaping from religious persecution. They led a simple farming life.

SOUTH AND CENTRAL AMERICA

After the overthrow of the Aztec and Inca Empires, Spanish and Portuguese settlers began to colonize South and Central America.

Spaniard

Inca

1600 1700 1750

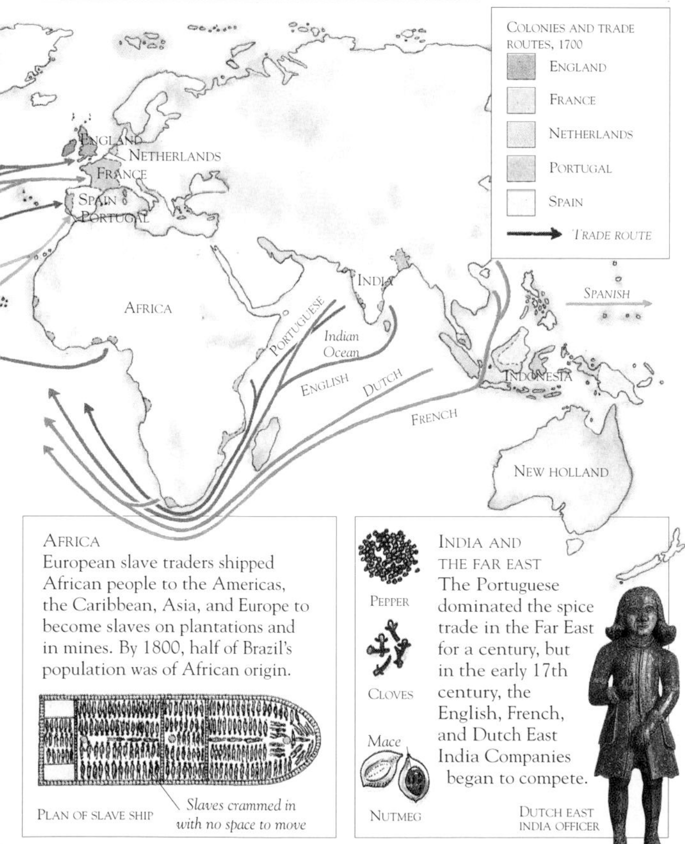

AFRICA

European slave traders shipped African people to the Americas, the Caribbean, Asia, and Europe to become slaves on plantations and in mines. By 1800, half of Brazil's population was of African origin.

PLAN OF SLAVE SHIP

Slaves crammed in with no space to move

INDIA AND THE FAR EAST

The Portuguese dominated the spice trade in the Far East for a century, but in the early 17th century, the English, French, and Dutch East India Companies began to compete.

DUTCH EAST INDIA OFFICER

Absolute rulers

DURING THE 17TH AND 18TH CENTURIES, Europe was dominated by monarchs who ruled with absolute power. This meant that they had total control over every aspect of their country, and could make reforms, raise taxes, or start wars without consulting anyone else.

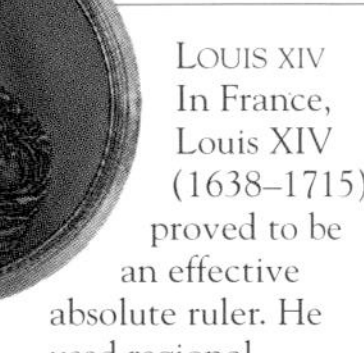
LOUIS XIV

LOUIS XIV
In France, Louis XIV (1638–1715) proved to be an effective absolute ruler. He used regional officials to rule the country, reduced the power of the nobles, and made France the most powerful country in Europe. However, because Louis led an extravagant life and waged expensive wars, he had to raise taxes, which were a burden to the ordinary people of France.

VERSAILLES
Louis brought many nobles to live in his palace at Versailles, where they could be easily controlled.

CHARLES I
The monarch of England traditionally ruled with the help of Parliament, but Charles I (1600–49) believed that he had the right to disregard Parliament. He ruled with absolute power for 11 years. Then in 1642, Charles' poor relationship with Parliament sparked off a civil war. Charles and his supporters were defeated, and the king was executed in 1649. England became a republic until 1660.

CHARLES I

EXECUTION OF CHARLES I

The divine right of kings

For hundreds of years, European monarchs claimed that they had been given the right to rule their countries by God. They believed that this meant they could rule as absolute monarchs, and that no one had the right to question their actions. All opposition to these monarchs was firmly suppressed.

Retaining power

- Powerful nobles were observed closely and kept busy with state ceremonies.
- Potential rebels were sent away on long diplomatic missions.

Peter the Great

The greatest of all the Russian tsars, Peter the Great (1672–1725) came to the throne in 1682. He brought western ideas, culture, and technology to Russia and reformed education, the civil service, the church, and the army. He warned Russian boyars (nobles) that they should not take their power for granted, and ordered that their traditional beards should be cut off to show that change was in the air.

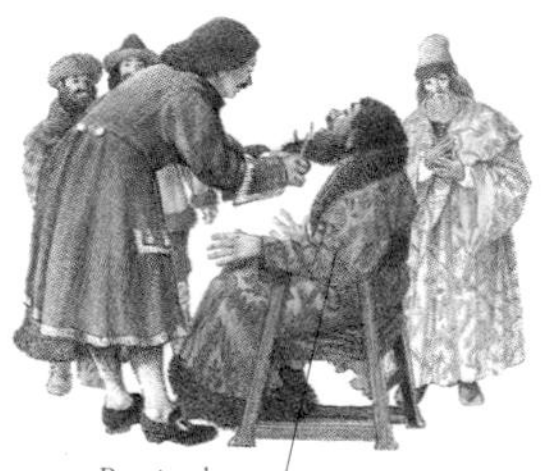

Russian boyar

Chinese figure

The Manchus

In 1644, the Manchu dynasty was founded in China. Early Manchu emperors crushed the resistance of the supporters of the preceding Ming dynasty and encouraged the arts and learning. The climax of the dynasty came with the reign of Quianlong (1736–96). He increased Chinese power in central Asia by defeating the Mongols and opening up trade routes to Europe.

Embroidered silk robe

K'ang Hsi, the second Manchu emperor

1750 TO 1900

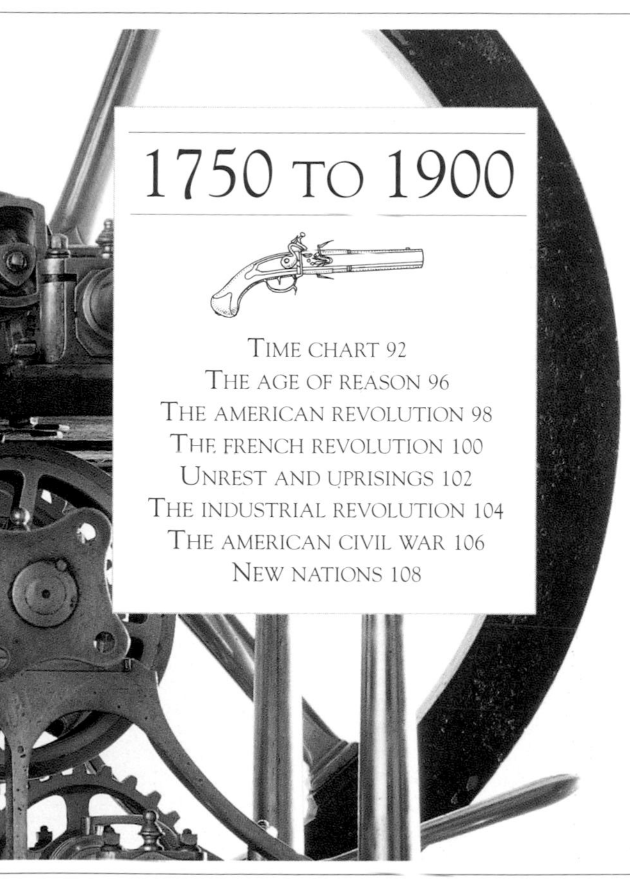

	1750	1765	1780
EVENTS	**1750** China conquers Tibet **1755** Earthquake at Lisbon, Portugal **1756–63** Seven Years War in Europe: Britain and Germany victorious **1757** Battle of Plassey: British conquer Bengal **1759** Battle of Quebec: British win control of Canada from French **1762** Catherine the Great (1729–96) begins reign in Russia **1763** Pontiac (1720–69) leads Native American uprising in North America	**1768** Ali Bey (d.1773) becomes ruler of independent Egypt **1769** Richard Arkwright (1732–92) builds first cotton factory **1770** James Cook (1728–79) reaches Australia ➡97 **1771** Russia conquers Crimea **1773** Boston Tea Party: North American colonists protest against taxes **1775–83** American Revolution ➡98, 99 **1776** Declaration of Independence, USA	**1787–89** United States Constitution and Bill of Rights written ➡99 **1788** British colony of New South Wales founded, Australia **1789** Storming of the Bastille begins French Revolution ➡100 **1791** Revolution in Haiti by Pierre Toussaint L'Ouverture (1743–1803) ➡99 **1792–1815** Napoleonic Wars in Europe led by Napoleon Bonaparte (1769–1821) ➡101
ARTS & ARCHITECTURE	**1751–86** *L'Encyclopédie*, the world's first encyclopedia, published, France ➡96 **1764** Eight-year-old Wolfgang Amadeus Mozart (1756–91) composes his first symphony	 MOZART	**1780** Johann Wolfgang von Goethe (1749–1832) pioneers Romantic movement in art and literature **1792** Mary Wollstonecraft (1759–97) writes *Vindication of the Rights of Women*
SCIENCE & INVENTION	**1752** Lightning conductor invented by Benjamin Franklin (1706–90) ➡97 **1757** Sextant invented by John Campbell (1720–90) ➡97	**1769** Rotary steam engine patented by James Watt (1736–1819) **1777** Antoine Lavoisier (1743–94) shows that air is made mainly of oxygen and nitrogen 	**1783** Étienne (1745–99) and Joseph (1740–1810) Montgolfier launch their hot-air balloon ➡97 **1792** Guillotine used for executions, France ➡100 GUILLOTINE, 1792

1795	1810	1825
1795 French Directoire government set up **1801** Union of Britain and Ireland **1804** British win control of Cape of Good Hope **1804** Napoleon becomes Emperor of France ➡101 **1805** Battle of Austerlitz: Napoleon defeats Russian and Austrian forces **1805** British admiral Horatio Nelson (1758–1805) destroys French fleet at Battle of Trafalgar ➡101 NAPOLEON	**1810–22** Many South American countries gain independence ➡103 **1812–14** Britain and USA at war **1814** Congress of Vienna restores European monarchies **1815** Battle of Waterloo: Napoleon defeated ➡101 **1821–29** Greek War of Independence from Turkey **1824–27** First Ashanti War between British and Ashanti of Gold Coast	**1830** British and Boers clash in South Africa **1830** French invade Algeria **1830** July Revolution overthrows Charles X (1757–1836) of France **1832** First Reform Act extends voting rights in Britain **1836** Great Trek of Boer farmers to establish independent Transvaal, South Africa **1836** Texas wins independence from Mexico **1837** Victoria (1819–1901) becomes Queen of England
1790 William Wordsworth (1770–1850) and Samuel Coleridge (1772–1834) found the English Romantic movement **1800** John Constable (1776–1837) pioneers painting outdoors	**1810** Greek revival architecture becomes popular in western Europe **1812** Brothers Jakob (1785–1863) and Wilhelm (1786–1859) Grimm publish their collection of fairy tales PASSENGER RAILWAY, 1825	**1832** Goethe completes *Faust* **1834** Munich Glypothek, first purpose-built museum, completed **1836–7** Charles Dickens (1812–70) publishes his first novel, *The Pickwick Papers*
1796 First vaccination given by Edward Jenner (1749–1823) **1800** Battery invented by Alessandro Volta (1745–1827) **1803** Steam locomotive invented by Richard Trevithick (1771–1883)	**1812** Tin can invented by Nicolas Appert (1750–1841) **1816** Stethoscope invented by René Laënnec (1781–1826) **1821** Electric motor invented by Michael Faraday (1791–1867) ➡105	**1825** First passenger railway opens, England ➡105 **1827** Photography pioneered by Joseph-Nicéphore Niepce (1765–1833) **1839** Louis Daguerre (1789–1851) develops his photographic technique

Time Chart

	1840	1850	1860
EVENTS	**1840** Treaty of Waitingi: British return ancient Maori land rights **1842** Treaty of Nanking opens Chinese ports to British trade and gives Hong Kong to Britain **1846** Potato famine begins, Ireland ➡103 **1846–48** Mexican–American War: USA victorious **1847** Bantus defeated by British in southern Africa **1848** California Gold Rush **1848** Year of revolutions in Europe ➡102	DAVID LIVINGSTONE  **1851** Australian Gold Rush **1853** US forces Japan to open up to foreign trade **1853–56** Crimean War: Britain and France defeat Russia **1855** David Livingstone (1813–73) reaches Victoria Falls, sparking off European exploration of African interior **1857** Indian Mutiny: Indians rebel against British	**1860–70** Maoris fight settlers in New Zealand **1861–65** American Civil War ➡106, 107 **1864** International Red Cross founded **1866** Austro–Prussian War: Austria defeated **1867** Dominion of Canada created **1867** Mexicans force French to withdraw from Mexico
ARTS & ARCHITECTURE	**1847** *Jane Eyre*, by Charlotte Brontë (1816–55), published CRYSTAL PALACE, 1851 	**1851** Crystal Palace built to house the Great Exhibition, celebrating the "Industry of All Nations", London **1856** Gustave Flaubert (1821–80) completes *Madame Bovary*	**1862** *Les Misérables*, by Victor Hugo (1802–85), published **1865** Lewis Carroll (1832–98) writes *Alice's Adventures in Wonderland* **1869** Suez Canal opens
SCIENCE & INVENTION	**1840** Postage stamps introduced in Britain ➡104 **1842** General anaesthetic first used by American surgeon Crawford Long (1815–78) **1845** First pneumatic tyres used, Scotland	**1856** First internal combustion engine developed in Italy and set up in Florence railway station **1859** *The Origin of Species*, by Charles Darwin (1809–82), published	**1862** First plastic invented by Alexander Parkes (1813–90) **1865** Antiseptic surgery first practised by Joseph Lister (1827–1912) ➡105 **1866** Dynamite invented by Alfred Nobel (1833–96)

1870	1880	1890
1870–71 Franco–Prussian War: France defeated **1871** Britain legalizes trade unions **1871** Otto von Bismarck (1815–98) unites German Empire ➡108 **1872** Samurai's feudal control in Japan ends **1876** Battle of Little Bighorn: Native Americans defeat US army **1879** Zulu War: British defeat Zulus, South Africa	**1881** First Boer War: Boers rebel against British rule, South Africa **1883** Volcano erupts on island of Krakatoa, Java **1884** Berlin Conference decides colonial divisions in Africa ➡109 **1885** Indian National Congress Party founded **1886** Gold discovered in South Africa ZULU WARRIOR, 1879	**1890** Battle of Wounded Knee: last massacre of Native Americans in USA **1893** New Zealand becomes first country to give women the vote **1894–95** Chinese–Japanese War: Japanese are victorious and occupy Korea **1895–96** Italy and Ethiopia at war: Ethiopia wins **1898** Spanish–American War: USA victorious **1899** Boxer rebellion of Chinese peasants **1899–1902** Second Boer War: Britain wins control of South Africa
1874 First exhibition of Impressionist painters, including Claude Monet (1840–1926), Paris, France **1874** Paris Opera House completed, France **1876** Mark Twain (1835–1910) writes *Tom Sawyer*	**1884** First skyscraper, 10 floors high, is built in Chicago, USA **1886** Statue of Liberty unveiled in New York Harbor, USA **1889** Eiffel Tower built, Paris, France EIFFEL TOWER, 1889	**1891** *Tess of the D'Urbervilles*, by Thomas Hardy (1840–1928) published **1894** Rudyard Kipling (1865–1936) writes *The Jungle Book* **1895** Art Nouveau style of decoration becomes fashionable
1876 Telephone invented by Alexander Graham Bell (1847–1922) **1879** Light bulb invented, England and USA	**1884** First underground railway opens, London, England **1885** Louis Pasteur (1822–95) produces vaccine against rabies **1885** Motor car invented by Karl Benz (1844–1929)	**1895** Motion pictures shown in public for the first time by inventors Auguste (1862–1954) and Louis (1864–1948) Lumière **1895** Wireless telegraph invented by Guglielmo Marconi (1874–1937)

THE AGE OF REASON

IN A MOVEMENT KNOWN as the Enlightenment, scientists and philosophers began to challenge accepted beliefs. They put forward new ideas about justice and liberty, which inspired later political revolutions.

NEWTON'S TELESCOPE, 1668

ENLIGHTENMENT FIGURES

NAME	DATES	INFORMATION
Isaac Newton	1642–1727	British scientist who worked out the law of gravity and discovered that white light is made up of many colours.
Voltaire	1694–1778	French writer who criticized governments and churchmen for their rigid thinking. He was twice imprisoned for his radical writings.
Carolus Linnaeus	1707–1778	Swedish naturalist who devised a way of classifying plants according to their shared features, a system still used today.
Denis Diderot	1713–1784	French writer who helped to compile the first encyclopedia, which collected together many Enlightenment ideas.

AGRICULTURAL CHANGES

In the 18th century, farmers began to create new strains of livestock and used crop rotation to preserve soil quality.

Basic tools like this changed little during the 18th century

HORSE-DRAWN PLOUGH, 1763

Coulter cuts vertically through the soil

Science

Enlightenment thinkers believed the key to understanding the world was science, rather than religion. Scientists relied on new methods of careful observation and experimentation. They made great advances and came up with many discoveries, from steam engines to vaccination against disease, from hot-air balloons to lightning conductors.

Sliding focus

Enlightenment books

- *The Social Contract* by French writer Jean-Jacques Rousseau (1712–78) inspired revolutionaries in France and America.
- The writings of French philosopher Montesquieu (1689–1755) influenced new constitutions such as the United States Constitution.

Cook's voyages

The South Seas

British navigator Captain James Cook (1728–79) made three voyages to Australia, New Zealand, and many South Pacific islands. Cook looked after his crews well, keeping them healthy by giving them fresh vegetables and fresh lime juice to ward off scurvy.

Limes

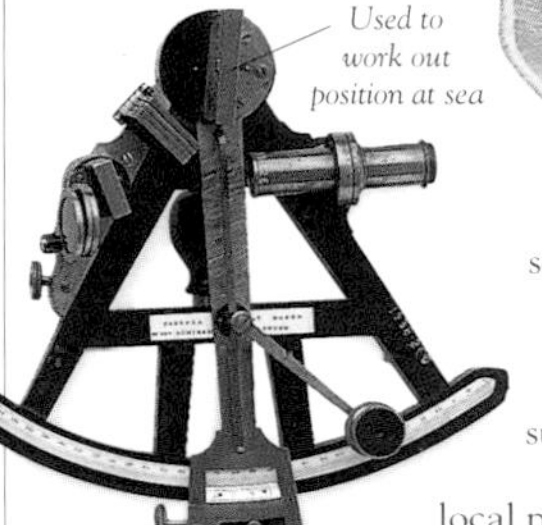

Used to work out position at sea

Sextant

Science at sea

Cook took a scientific approach to exploration. Scientists on Cook's voyages surveyed the coasts and investigated local plants and wildlife.

Cook meets Pacific islanders

THE AMERICAN REVOLUTION

DURING THE 1760s, the British government began to tax North American colonists, even though the colonists were given no representation in the British Parliament. The colonists refused to pay, and war broke out in 1775. In 1783, the colonists defeated the British and won their independence.

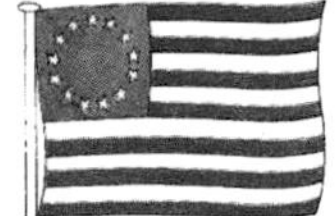

STARS AND STRIPES
The first US flag had 13 stars and 13 stripes for the 13 original states.

REVOLUTIONARY LEADERS		
NAME	DATES	INFORMATION
George Washington	1732–1799	Army commander who was elected first President of the United States in 1789.
Thomas Jefferson	1743–1826	Helped to draft the Declaration of Independence; became third President.
Benjamin Franklin	1706–1790	Negotiated peace with Britain; helped to draft the Constitution.

Washington

US flag

CROSSING THE DELAWARE
On Christmas night 1776, Washington made a daring crossing of the Delaware River, taking the British by surprise.

IMPORTANT BATTLES

- In 1775, the Americans won the war's first battle, at Lexington.
- In 1777, British forces surrendered at Saratoga.
- In 1781, the British surrendered at Yorktown, leading to the end of the war.

THE AMERICANS
With poor organization, the Americans sometimes found it difficult to supply their troops. However, they knew the local terrain and could get reinforcements easily.

THE BRITISH
Some British leaders moved their troops deliberately slowly, because they wanted a political solution to the war.

CONSTITUTION

Under the new Constitution, the federal government had clear power. A Bill of Rights and other systems maintained balanced power and protected individual rights, such as freedom of speech and trial by jury.

TOUSSAINT L'OUVERTURE

In 1791, the slaves of the Caribbean island of Sainte Domingue (Haiti) organized a rebellion, led by Pierre Toussaint l'Ouverture (1743–1803), a former slave. The revolutionaries made Toussaint governor of the island. Eventually, Toussaint was captured by Napoleon, who reintroduced slavery.

TOUSSAINT L'OUVERTURE

THE FRENCH REVOLUTION

THE PEOPLE OF 18TH-CENTURY FRANCE had long suffered from high taxes, bad harvests, and limitations on their freedom. On 14 July 1789, an angry crowd stormed the Bastille prison in Paris, starting the French Revolution.

LOUIS XVI
After trying to make concessions to the people, King Louis XVI (b.1754) was executed in January 1793.

MARIE ANTOINETTE
Hated because of her lavish lifestyle, the queen (b.1755) was executed in October 1793.

THE TERROR
During the Reign of Terror, opponents of revolutionary leader Maximilien Robespierre (1758–94) were ruthlessly guillotined. Robespierre himself was executed in 1794.

Napoleon

A brilliant general in the revolutionary wars, Napoleon Bonaparte (1769–1821) wanted to rule France himself. In 1804, he made himself Emperor and then launched a series of ambitious military campaigns to conquer much of Europe.

NAPOLEONIC WARS
By 1809, Napoleon had conquered most of Europe. However, the British defeated him at Trafalgar in 1805, and his 1812 Russian campaign ended in a disastrous retreat with many French troops losing their lives.

NAPOLEON'S ARMY
The army was run with great efficiency. Promotion was according to ability, rather than money or family connections. Troops were usually well provided with food and other supplies.

THE NAPOLEONIC CODE

A new legal system was set up, which is still the basis of French law. The code included:

- Freedom of religion.
- Equality for all before the law.
- Abolition of class privileges.

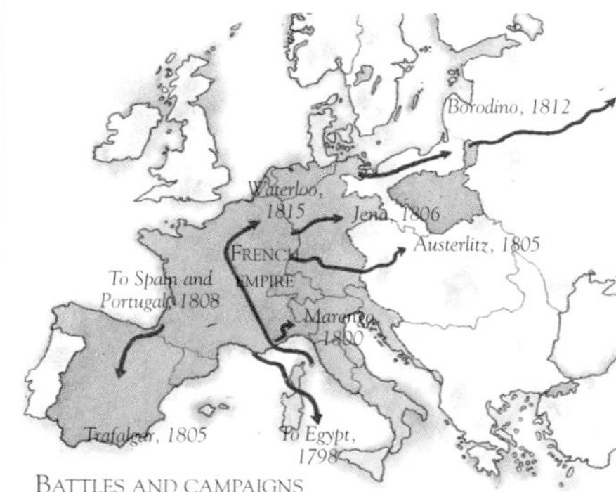

BATTLES AND CAMPAIGNS
In 1815, the combined efforts of the Prussians and British at Waterloo, Belgium, finally brought about Napoleon's final defeat. Napoleon was exiled to the South Atlantic island of St Helena, where he died.

Unrest and uprisings

THE FIRST HALF of the 19th century saw uprisings and revolutions in many countries. In Europe, people rose up against oppressive regimes, while in South America, the struggle for independence began.

KARL MARX
German writer Karl Marx (1818–83) pressed for social reforms.

Europe

Bad harvests, famine, unemployment, and economic depression made many people discontented in Europe in the 1840s, and they began to rise up against the governments in power. Most of the revolutions were defeated, but in many cases the rulers had to make some concessions to the people, such as granting constitutions.

Prussian soldier

PRUSSIAN REVOLT
The Prussian uprising led to rebellions in other German-speaking states and pressure for a united Germany.

1848 – YEAR OF REVOLUTIONS

AREA	EVENTS
France	Workers and middle classes bring down King Louis Philippe (1773–1848).
Prussia	Uprising is quelled by King Frederick William IV (1795–1861); constitution is granted.
Austria	Revolution forces Prince Metternich (1773–1859) to flee to London.
Italian states	Sicilian revolt spreads north, forcing Austrians out of Italy and Pope into temporary exile.
Hungary	Uprising against Austrian rule crushed with the help of Russian forces.

FAMINE AND EMIGRATION

In Ireland in 1846, a disease destroyed the potato crop. Over a million people who relied upon potatoes as a staple food died of starvation. As a result, many people decided to emigrate to North America. Many German people also left for the USA at this time.

South America

Spain and Portugal had ruled over much of South America for 150 years. Encouraged by the American and French Revolutions, South American nations began to seek self-government in the early 19th century. The new nations created in this period have survived to the present day.

VENEZUELA 1821
COLOMBIA 1819
GUIANA
BRAZIL (Portuguese) 1822
PERU 1821
BOLIVIA 1825
URUGUAY 1828
CHILE 1818
ARGENTINA 1816

INDEPENDENCE

SPANISH COLONIES (WITH INDEPENDENCE DATES)

DUTCH, FRENCH, AND BRITISH COLONIES

INDEPENDENCE LEADERS

- Simon Bolivar (1783–1830) helped many countries to independence and hoped to unite all of South America.
- José de San Martin (1778–1850) led uprisings in Argentina, Peru, and Chile.

LIBERATION

As in many other South American states, it took several attempts before the Spanish were expelled from Chile. Finally, in 1818, people danced under their new national flag.

THE INDUSTRIAL REVOLUTION

IN THE 19TH CENTURY, new technology began to transform the way people worked and lived their lives. Better transport, new cities, and large factories with machines powered by water wheels or steam engines began to appear. This industrial revolution began in Britain, but soon spread across Europe and to the USA.

POSTAGE ONE PENNY

PENNY POST
The first stamps were used in Britain in 1840.

Train transporting materials

Railway bridge

Factory

Canal barge

Small houses for workers

A NEW WAY OF LIFE
Huge numbers of people began to move away from the countryside and into the towns so that they could find work in the new factories.

Industrial revolution innovations

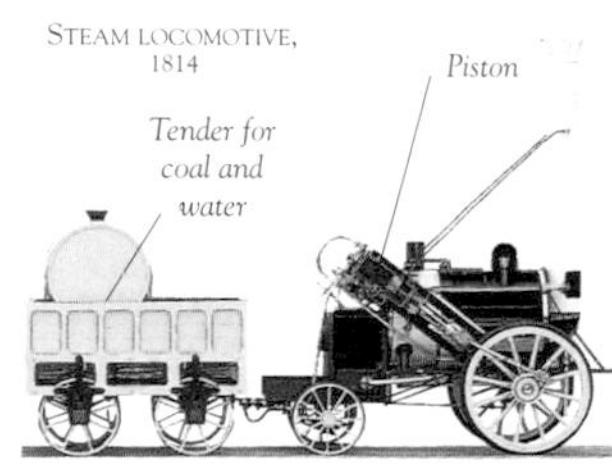

Steam locomotive, 1814

Steam engines and railways

The steam engine was developed in the 18th century to pump water out of mines and to power factory machinery. In the early 19th century, steam engines were first used to power railway locomotives, and a new era of transport had begun. Soon, steam locomotives were hauling both goods and passengers.

Medical advances

There were many developments in medicine, from the use of ether as an anaesthetic, to the invention of the stethoscope. Antiseptics helped to reduce the risk of infections that had previously been a common cause of death after surgery.

Ether inhaler, 1847

Electricity

In 1821, British scientist Michael Faraday (1791–1867) invented the electric motor, but electricity was not commonly used in the home until the 20th century.

Coil from Faraday's transformer

Industrial machinery

One of the first businesses to use machines on a large scale was the textile industry. In the past, spinning and weaving had been done on small machines in people's homes. Large steam-powered machines had to be housed in factories, and so textile workers now had to go out to work.

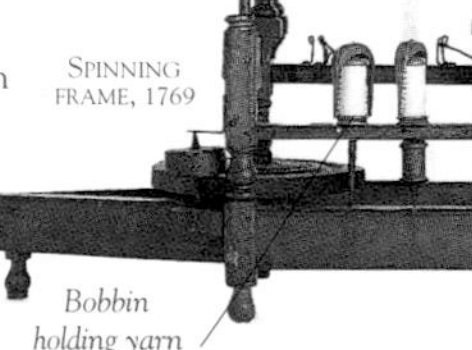

Spinning frame, 1769

THE AMERICAN CIVIL WAR

IN 1861, WAR BROKE OUT between the northern and southern states of the USA. The South feared the growing economic power of the industrial North, and resented their efforts to ban slavery. The war lasted until the South surrendered in 1865.

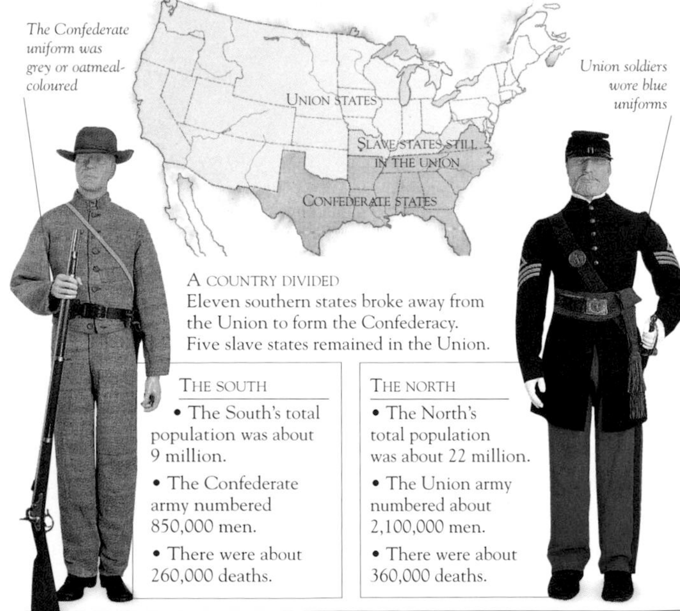

The Confederate uniform was grey or oatmeal-coloured

Union soldiers wore blue uniforms

A COUNTRY DIVIDED
Eleven southern states broke away from the Union to form the Confederacy. Five slave states remained in the Union.

THE SOUTH

- The South's total population was about 9 million.
- The Confederate army numbered 850,000 men.
- There were about 260,000 deaths.

THE NORTH

- The North's total population was about 22 million.
- The Union army numbered about 2,100,000 men.
- There were about 360,000 deaths.

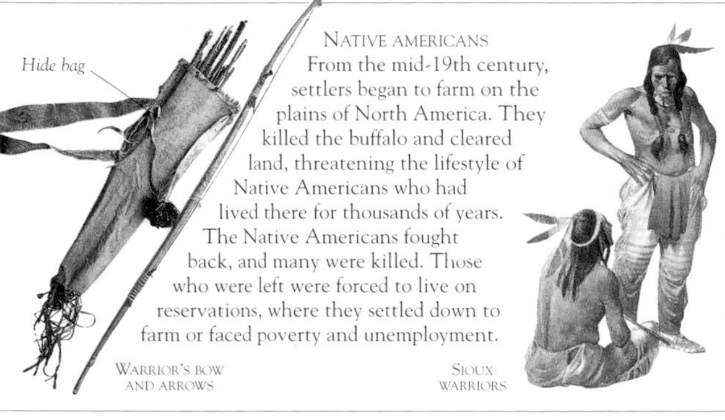

Native Americans

From the mid-19th century, settlers began to farm on the plains of North America. They killed the buffalo and cleared land, threatening the lifestyle of Native Americans who had lived there for thousands of years. The Native Americans fought back, and many were killed. Those who were left were forced to live on reservations, where they settled down to farm or faced poverty and unemployment.

Warrior's bow and arrows

Sioux warriors

Flag of the Confederacy

After the North won the war, there were many reforms in the South. Slavery was abolished, free schooling was introduced, and taxes were made fairer.

A modern war

In many ways, the Civil War was the first modern war. Railways and iron ships were used to transport troops, field telegraphs relayed messages from commanders, and newspaper reporters sent back reports and photographs from the battlefields.

Glass-plate camera, 1860s

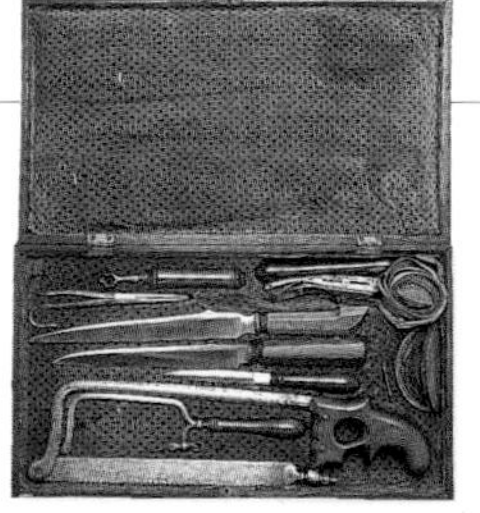

Instrument case of military surgeon, 1860s

New nations

In the 19th century, the maps of Africa and Europe began to take their modern shape. Italy and Germany became nations in their own right, and European powers began to carve up Africa.

Italy and Germany

Sardinian King Victor Emmanuel II (1820–78) drove the Austrians out of Italy, and united all of Italy except Venice and Rome in 1860. German unification centred around Prussia, under the leadership of King William I (1797–1888).

Italian national flag with the arms of Savoy

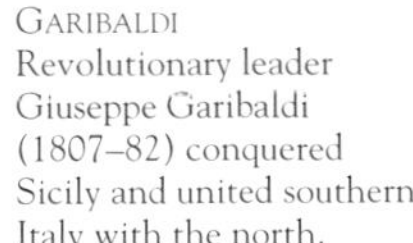

Garibaldi
Revolutionary leader Giuseppe Garibaldi (1807–82) conquered Sicily and united southern Italy with the north.

The new Germany

- Germany was made up of 38 states before unification in 1871.
- By 1914, Germany's army was 12 times the size of the British army.
- Germany built up a university system that trained some of the world's best scientists and engineers.

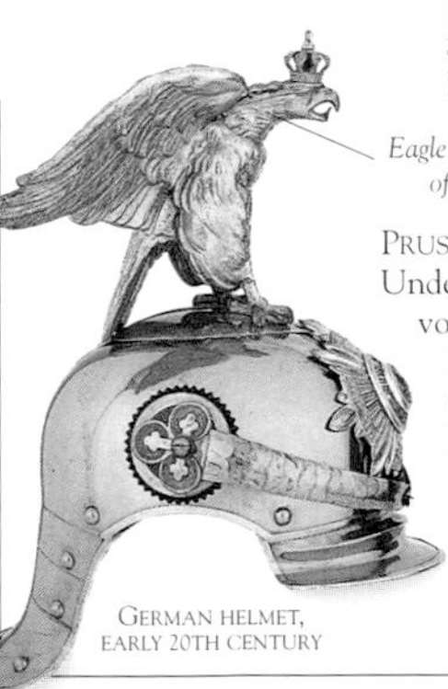

Eagle, the symbol of Prussia

German helmet, early 20th century

Prussian might
Under Chancellor Otto von Bismarck (1815–98), Prussia became one of the strongest powers in Europe and was able to dominate the other German states. In 1871, King William was proclaimed Emperor of Germany.

The scramble for Africa

In the last 30 years of the 19th century, European powers competed in taking over vast territories in Africa. They wanted cheap African raw materials for industries at home. In 1884, European leaders held a conference in Berlin to agree on their claims to African land.

COCOA
Tropical regions of Africa proved a good environment for growing cocoa.

AFRICA DIVIDED

- FRENCH
- BRITISH
- GERMAN
- PORTUGUESE
- BELGIAN
- SPANISH
- ITALIAN
- ANGLO-EGYPTIAN CONDOMINIUM

COTTON
In the late 19th century, cotton was a vital raw material for expanding European textile mills.

COFFEE
Plantations were set up all over southern and central Africa, producing coffee for export to Europe.

Diamond

DIAMONDS AND GOLD
The search for wealth in the form of gold and diamonds attracted many European adventurers to Africa.

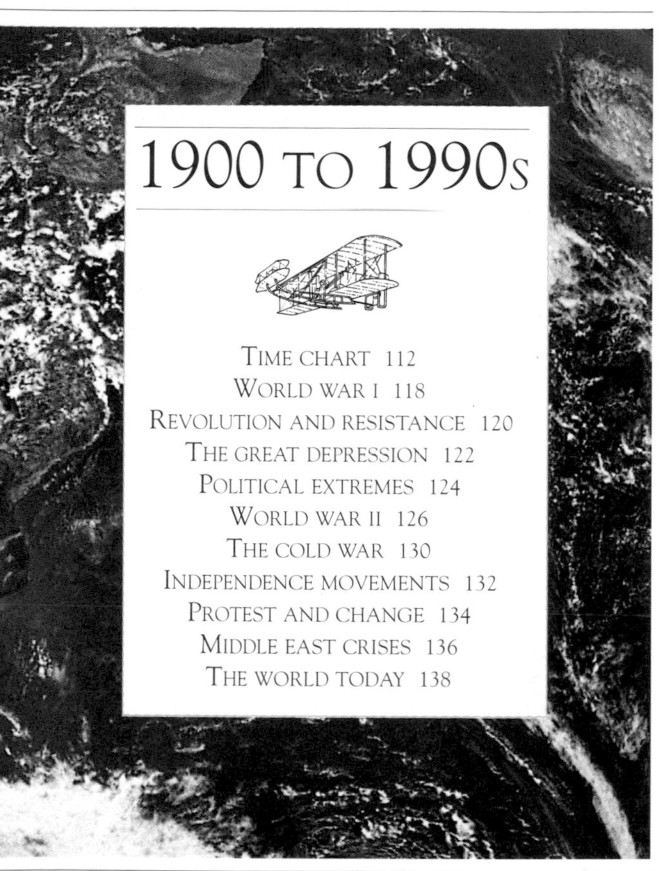

1900 TO 1990s

	1900	1905	1910
EVENTS	**1900** Expansion of German navy begins arms race with Britain **1901** Commonwealth of Australia proclaimed **1901** Peace of Peking ends Boxer Rebellion in China **1903** First Tour de France bicycle race **1903** Votes for Women Movement formed in Britain by Emmeline Pankhurst (1858–1928) **1904** Entente Cordiale (friendly understanding) between Britain and France **1904–5** Russo–Japanese War: Japan victorious	**1905** Union of South Africa formed from former Boer republics **1905** Workers' uprising put down by imperial troops, Russia **1905** World's largest diamond found, South Africa **1906** Earthquake hits San Francisco, USA **1907** Oil discovered, Iran **1909** Robert Peary (1856–1920) claims to have reached the North Pole	AMUNDSEN AT SOUTH POLE, 1911 **1911** Chinese revolution overthrows Manchu dynasty **1911** Roald Amundsen (1872–1928) reaches South Pole **1912** African National Congress formed ➡121 **1912–13** Balkan Wars: Greece, Serbia, Bulgaria, and Montenegro against Turkey **1914–18** World War I ➡118, 119
ARTS & ARCHITECTURE	**1903** *The Call of the Wild*, by Jack London (1876–1916) published **1904** Giacomo Puccini (1858–1924) writes *Madame Butterfly* SIGMUND FREUD	**1907** First comic strips appear in USA **1907** Pablo Picasso (1881–1973) leads Cubist movement in art **1908** First steel and glass building, AEG factory, Berlin	**1910** Paul Klee (1879–1940) pioneers abstract art movement **1913** Premiere of *The Rites of Spring* by Igor Stravinsky (1882–1971) causes riot in theatre **1914** Panama Canal opens
SCIENCE & INVENTION	**1900** *The Interpretation of Dreams*, by Sigmund Freud (1856–1939), published **1903** Orville (1871–1948) and Wilbur (1867–1912) Wright make the first powered flight, USA	**1905** Albert Einstein (1879–1955) develops his Special Theory of Relativity **1909** Chromosomes established as carriers of heredity	**1911** Cellophane first manufactured **1911** Ernest Rutherford (1871–1937) announces nuclear theory, that the atom contains a central nucleus **1914** Zip fasteners go on sale

1915	1920	1925
1915 Mohandas K. Gandhi (1869–1948) becomes leader of Indian National Congress Party ➡121 **1916** Easter Rising against British rule, Ireland ➡121 **1917** Revolt against French rule, Chad **1917** Russian Revolution ➡120, 121 **1918** Women gain vote in Britain **1918–21** Russian Civil War: Bolsheviks defeat anti-communists	**1920** Women gain vote in USA **1920–33** Prohibition of sale of alcohol in USA **1922** Discovery of tomb of Tutankhamun, Egypt **1922** Egypt wins independence from Britain **1923** Ireland wins partial independence from Britain ➡121 **1924** Josef Stalin (1879–1953) becomes leader of USSR TUTANKHAMUN'S TOMB FOUND, 1922	**1926** In Britain, a general strike almost brings the country to a standstill; it is defeated by police and army **1928** Mao Tse-tung (1893–1976) and Communists attempt to overthrow Chinese government led by Chiang Kai-shek (1887–1975) ➡124 **1929** Arabs attack Jews in Palestine in a conflict over use of the Wailing Wall, Jerusalem **1929** Leon Trotsky (1879–1940) exiled from USSR **1929** Wall Street Crash, USA ➡122
1915 *The Tramp*, starring Charlie Chaplin (1889–1977), wins international acclaim **1919** Bauhaus school of architecture and design founded in Germany	**1922** Completion of earthquake-proof hotel, Tokyo, designed by Frank Lloyd Wright (1867–1959) **1922** *The Waste Land*, by T. S. Eliot (1888–1965) published	**1927** Stan Laurel (1890–1965) and Oliver Hardy (1892–1957) make the first of several films together **1927** *The Jazz Singer*, the first "talkie" (feature film with sound) is released LAUREL AND HARDY
1915 First transcontinental telephone call **1915** Tractors introduced by Ford **1916** Tanks invented by William Tritton (1875–1946) as a British secret weapon	**1920** Regular radio broadcasting begins in USA **1922** Insulin first used for the treatment of diabetes **1924** Clarence Birdseye (1886–1956) experiments with quick-frozen foods	**1928** First TV broadcasts **1928** Jet engine invented by Frank Whittle (b.1907) **1928** Penicillium mould discovered by Alexander Fleming (1881–1955), leading to invention of antibiotics (1940)

	1930	1935	1940
EVENTS	**1930** Ras Tafari (1892–1975) is crowned Haile Selassie in Ethiopia **1931** Canada gains full independence from Britain **1931–33** Chinese–Japanese War: Japan victorious **1933** Adolf Hitler (1889–1945) becomes German Chancellor ➡125 **1934–35** Long March in China ➡124 WORLD WAR II AEROPLANES, 1939–45	**1935** Italy invades Ethiopia ➡125 **1936** Germany hosts Olympic Games in Berlin **1936** Italy signs alliance with Germany ➡125 **1936–39** Spanish Civil War ➡124 **1937** Japan and China at war **1938** Germany takes over Czechoslovakia ➡125 **1939** Germany invades Poland **1939–45** World War II ➡126, 127	**1940** Germany occupies Denmark, Norway, France, Belgium, and the Netherlands **1941** Allied troops overrun Italy's African colonies **1941** Germans move into eastern Europe **1941** Japanese planes attack US fleet at Pearl Harbor ➡126 **1941–42** Japan takes over American, British, and Dutch colonies in Indian and Pacific Oceans ➡127 **1944** Allies invade France and drive back Germans
ARTS & ARCHITECTURE	**1930** Salvador Dali (1904–84) pioneers the Surrealist movement in art **1930** The opera *The Rise and Fall of the City of Mahagonny* by Kurt Weill (1900–50) is performed **1931** Empire State Building built, New York	**1935** Musical theatre reaches its peak with first performance of *Porgy and Bess* by George Gershwin (1898–1937) **1936** Hoover Dam completed, USA ➡123	**1940** *Darkness at Noon* by Arthur Koestler (1905–83) describes life under Stalinism **1940** Duke Ellington (1899–1974) becomes popular as jazz pianist and composer
SCIENCE & INVENTION	**1931** Electron microscope invented by Ernst Ruska (1906–88) **1933–35** Radar invented in Britain and Germany **1934** Wallace Carothers (1896–1937) invents nylon	**1939** DDT insecticide first used to kill mosquitoes **1939** Igor Sikorsky (1889–1972) invents single rotor helicopter **1939** Jet aircraft built by Ernst Heinkel (1888–1958)	**1941** First aerosol cans **1942** Enrico Fermi (1901–54) builds first nuclear reactor, USA **1942** Rocket-propelled missile invented by Wernher von Braun (1912–77)

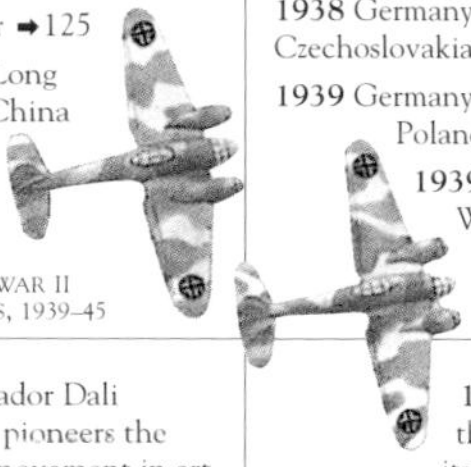

1945	1950	1955
1945 German forces surrender **1945** USA drops atomic bombs on Hiroshima and Nagasaki ➡127 **1947** India wins independence from Britain ➡132 **1948** State of Israel created ➡136 **1949** Germany split into East and West ➡128 **1949** Mao proclaims new Communist Republic of China **1949** NATO formed ➡130	ATOM BOMB, 1945 **1950** China occupies Tibet **1950** Group Area Act legalizes apartheid, South Africa **1950** US Senator Joseph McCarthy (1908–57) begins anti-communist "witch-hunts" **1950–53** Korean War ➡131 **1953** Tensing Norgay (1914–86) and Edmund Hillary (b.1919) are the first to climb Mount Everest, the world's highest mountain	**1955** Black people in Montgomery, Alabama, USA, boycott segregated buses **1955** Warsaw Pact formed ➡130 **1956** Hungarian uprising **1956** Suez Crisis: Egyptian troops force French and British to withdraw **1957** European Economic Community formed ➡129 **1957** Pass Laws in South Africa state that all non-whites must carry passes **1959** Revolution in Cuba brings Fidel Castro (b.1926) to power
1945 Abstract Expressionist style of art develops in USA, led by Jackson Pollock (1912–56) **1946** Jean Paul Sartre (1905–80), pioneer of the Existentialist movement, writes *Being and Nothingness*	**1950** Theatre of the Absurd developed by Samuel Beckett (1906–89) and Eugène Ionesco (1912–94) ELVIS PRESLEY	**1956** Rock and roll music reaches height of popularity with artists such as Elvis Presley (1935–77) **1957** Boris Pasternak (1890–1960) writes *Doctor Zhivago*
1945 First electronic computer developed **1947** Sound barrier first broken by Bell XI aircraft **1948** Invention of the transistor makes it possible to build smaller electronic equipment	**1953** Link between smoking and lung cancer established **1953** Structure of DNA discovered **1953–5** Polio vaccine developed **1954** Hydrogen bomb tested by the USA	**1955** Tefal company develops non-stick pans, France **1957** USSR launches first artificial satellite ➡131 **1958** Integrated circuit, or "silicon chip", invented

	1960	1966	1972
EVENTS	**1960** 17 African colonies gain independence ➡133 **1961** Berlin Wall built **1963** President John F. Kennedy (b.1917) is assassinated **1964** ANC leader Nelson Mandela (b.1918) is jailed in South Africa ➡133 **1965** Civil rights leader Malcolm X (b.1925) is assassinated ➡134 **1965–75** Vietnam War ➡131	 MARTIN LUTHER KING **1966** Cultural Revolution begins in China ➡135 **1967** Six Day War between Israelis and Arabs ➡137 **1968** Anti-communist uprising in Prague crushed ➡134 **1968** Civil rights leader Martin Luther King (b.1929) is assassinated ➡134 **1968** Civil war begins in Northern Ireland **1968** Student riots in Paris	**1972** Independent state of Bangladesh founded **1973** Arab–Israeli War ➡137 **1974** US President Richard Nixon (1913–95) resigns over Watergate scandal **1975** Juan Carlos (b.1938) becomes Spanish King after death of Francisco Franco (b.1892) **1976** North and South Vietnam reunited after 22 years of separation **1976** Riots in black townships across South Africa
ARTS & ARCHITECTURE	**1960** Pop Art pioneered by Roy Lichtenstein (b.1923) and Andy Warhol (1928–87) in USA **1962** British pop group The Beatles have their first hit, *Love Me Do*	**1967** Gabriel Garciá Márquez (b.1928) writes *One Hundred Years of Solitude* 	**1972** Sydney Opera House opened, Australia **1976** Punk rock emerges in England, led by British group, the Sex Pistols **1977** Pompidou Centre completed, Paris SYDNEY OPERA HOUSE, 1972
SCIENCE & INVENTION	**1960** Laser invented for use in precision cutting and surgery, USA **1961** Yuri Gagarin (1934–68) is first man in space ➡131 **1965** Space probe sends back first pictures from Mars	**1967** Christiaan Barnard (b.1922) performs first heart transplant **1969** Concorde becomes the first supersonic passenger aircraft **1969** First Moon landing ➡131	**1973** Videotex (text transmission via television) is developed **1975** Soviet and US spacecraft link up in space **1975** Video recorder launched by Sony Corporation

1978	1984	1990
1978 Margaret Thatcher (b.1925) becomes Britain's first woman prime minister **1979** Camp David peace treaty between Egypt and Israel ➡137 **1979** Iranian Revolution **1979** Marxist Sandinistas take power in Nicaragua **1980** Lech Walesa (b.1943) leads Solidarity trade union in Poland **1980–88** Iran–Iraq War ➡133 **1982** Falklands War: Britain defeats Argentine forces **1983** Famine in Ethiopia	**1984** New Zealand declared a nuclear-free zone **1989** Chinese security forces put down pro-democracy movement in Beijing's Tiananmen Square **1989** Communist governments overthrown in eastern Europe ➡138 **1989** Martial law imposed in Lhasa, Tibet, by Chinese FAMINE IN ETHIOPIA, 1983	**1990** Gulf War begins ➡137 **1990** Namibia gains independence from South Africa **1991** Break-up of Soviet Union ➡138 **1992** Civil war begins, former Yugoslavia **1992** Muslim–Hindu riots, India **1994** ANC wins South Africa's first free elections **1994** IRA ceasefire begins in Northern Ireland **1994** PLO gains autonomy in Gaza strip
1978 AT&T Building, New York, by Philip Johnson (b.1906), and Portland Building, Oregon, by Michael Graves (b.1934), pioneer the style of postmodernism **1978** Disco music and dancing become popular	**1986** Hong Kong and Shanghai Bank, Hong Kong, opens, designed by Norman Foster (b.1935)	**1994** Channel Tunnel between England and France opened **1995** Artist Christo (b.1935) wraps German Reichstag building in silver fabric
1978 First "test-tube" baby born, England ➡139 **1980** Smallpox is eradicated **1981** First reuseable space shuttle launched in USA **1981** Solar-powered aircraft crosses English Channel	**1984** French and US scientists identify AIDS-related HIV virus **1984** Genetic fingerprinting, a technique for identifying people by their unique DNA pattern, is pioneered	**1990s** Computers all over the world are linked via telephone lines to create the Internet **1990s** Interactive CD-ROMs are introduced **1995** US space shuttle Challenger docks with Russian space station Mir

World War I

In July 1914, war broke out between Serbia and Austria after a Serbian nationalist murdered the heir to the Austrian throne. Most European powers had an alliance with one of the two sides, so they were soon drawn into the crisis. The Great War grew to a scale never seen before. By 1918, the death toll had reached 20 million.

Infantryman
Most of the fighting was done on the ground, by men like this French soldier.

A new kind of war

The war was very different from previous conflicts. It involved the whole adult populations of many nations. Vast numbers of men were called up to fight, while women took over men's jobs or worked in armaments factories. Poison gas and tanks were used for the first time, and aeroplanes were used for observation, bombing, and fighting.

Propeller
Top wing
Observer seat
National marking

BE 2B
BOMBER, 1914

World War I battles

Battle	Information
Tannenberg, August 1914	Germans halt the advance of the Russians, taking some 125,000 men prisoner.
The Marne, September 1914	Last mobile action of the war in the west; French and British push back the Germans.
Gallipoli, April 1915	Australia, New Zealand, and Britain suffer many casualties trying to take Constantinople.
Passchendaele, July 1917	British and Canadians make a small advance, but at the cost of more than 250,000 lives.
Cambrai, November 1917	British tanks break through German lines, causing a German collapse.

Sandbags

Wooden props

Barbed wire

German troops run into No-Man's Land

TRENCH WARFARE
Much of the war in northern Europe was fought between parallel lines of trenches. Soldiers were ordered to charge into the area of No-Man's Land between the trenches to push back the enemy.

WESTERN FRONTS
Countries that fought with Germany and Austria were known as the Central Powers; their opponents became known as the Allies. The USA entered the war on the Allied side at the end of 1917.

THE HUMAN COST
4.9 million Allied troops died in battle and 113 million were wounded. The Central Powers lost 3.1 million troops in battle and 8.4 million were wounded.

650,000 German

420,000 British

195,000 French

BATTLE OF THE SOMME CASUALTIES

Revolution and Resistance

Low pay in the cities, poor conditions for farmers, and the Tsar's tyrannical rule led to discontent in early 20th-century Russia. Workers began to demand their rights, and in 1917, revolution erupted. By the end of the year, the Soviet Union, the world's first communist nation, had been founded.

The tsar and his family
Nicholas II (1868–1918) was forced to abdicate in 1917. He and his family were shot dead by the Bolsheviks in 1918.

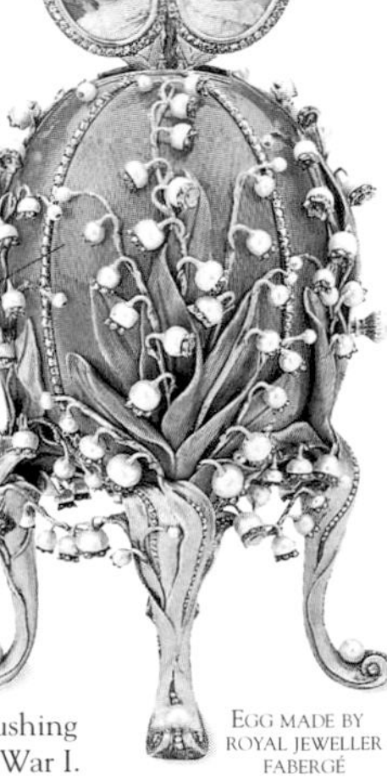

Pictures of the royal family

Inlaid with precious stones

Egg made by royal jeweller Fabergé

Red and white

- Known as the Reds, the Communist Bolsheviks were led by Vladimir Lenin (1870–1924).
- After the revolution, anti-Bolshevists became known as White Russians.

Royal riches
Palaces filled with art treasures made a stark contrast with the living conditions of the poor. These conditions worsened dramatically following crushing Russian defeats in World War I.

Winter Palace

Cruiser Aurora fires blanks at the palace

SIEGE OF THE WINTER PALACE
After the Tsar abdicated, a temporary government was set up. But discontent continued and in October 1917, the Bolsheviks besieged the government in the Winter Palace in St Petersburg. Faced by little opposition, the Bolsheviks took power.

Communist hammer and sickle symbol

THE NEW REGIME
The communists gave more land to peasants and gave workers control of their factories.

RESISTANCE MOVEMENTS AROUND THE WORLD

PLACE	DATE	INFORMATION
South Africa	1912	The white minority took over most of the land in South Africa, and restricted the rights of non-white South Africans. In 1912, the African National Congress (ANC) was founded to defend the rights of black and coloured people.
Ireland	1916–1922	Britain had promised the Irish Home Rule, but it was delayed because of World War I. Irish nationalists took over Dublin in the Easter Rising, but Britain defeated the rebels. The Irish Free State was finally created in southern Ireland in 1922.
India	1919–1947	The campaign for independence in India led to strikes and riots. After British soldiers massacred more than 300 protesters at Amritsar in 1919, nationalist leader Mohandas K. Gandhi (1869–1948) began his campaign of passive resistance to British rule .

THE GREAT DEPRESSION

THE NEW YORK Stock Exchange crashed dramatically in October 1929, as shareholders panicked and sold their shares. Many people lost their jobs, their savings, their businesses, and even their homes. Meanwhile, there was a slump in agriculture, as over-production led to falling prices. The economic crisis spread to most parts of the world, causing poverty for millions.

THE DUST BOWL
In the west and midwest of the USA, many farmers were forced to abandon their land because low rainfall made the soil turn to barren dust.

POVERTY AND HUNGER
The problem of unemployment was severe in the large cities of the USA. Even before the Stock Market crash, many businesses had already failed due to over-priced shares and over-production. Particularly badly hit were the mining, railway, and textile industries. As a result, thousands of families could no longer afford to eat.

Queuing to receive free food

THE SOVIET UNION

Soviet leader Josef Stalin (1879–1953) introduced his Five Year Plan to force expansion in industry and agriculture.

- Peasants who objected to giving their lands to the State were imprisoned or killed.
- In spite of the industrial expansion, economic chaos, famine, and poverty were widespread in the early 1930s.

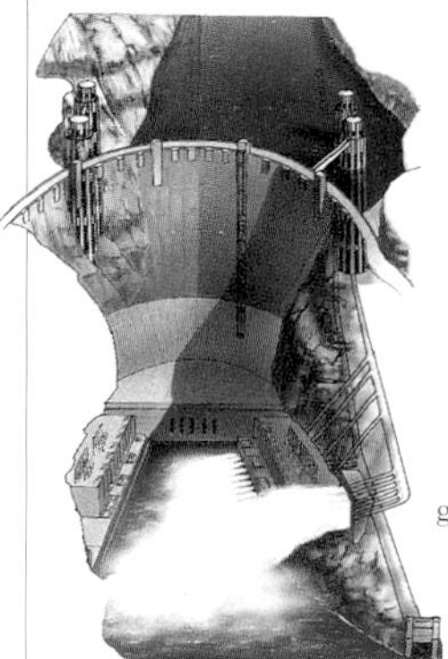

HOOVER DAM, 1936

THE NEW DEAL

New US President Franklin D. Roosevelt (1882–1945) tackled the Depression with a policy known as the New Deal. This included a programme of public works, such as forest planting and hydro-electric schemes, designed to get unemployed people back to work.

EUROPE

Europe was badly hit by the Depression.

- There was a sharp fall in industrial production, and trade fell to 35 per cent of its 1929 rate.
- Currencies declined in value and prices in the shops rose.

THE MOVIES

The film industry was one of the few businesses that flourished during the Depression years. The new talkies provided people with a cheap distraction from their troubles.

TECHNICOLOR MOVIE CAMERA

200,000,000 German Mark note

MAD MONEY

Rising prices made currencies such as the German Mark virtually worthless. At Tenino in the USA, a shortage of cash led to wooden banknotes.

POLITICAL EXTREMES

IN MANY COUNTRIES, governments were blamed for the hardships of the Depression. New strong governments led by dictators dealt successfully with the economic problems, but their extreme beliefs and repressive regimes led to terrible suffering, and ultimately to war.

SPANISH CIVIL WAR
In 1936, Francisco Franco (1892–1975) led a rebellion against the government. By 1939, the government and its communist supporters were defeated. Franco ruled Spain until his death.

Communism

In a communist system, profit-seeking and speculation do not exist, so in theory there can be no economic crises. Under Stalin, industry flourished in the Soviet Union, while in China, the Communists led by Mao Tse-tung (1893–1976) struggled to take power.

THE LONG MARCH
Expelled by the ruling Kuomintang party, Mao and his allies marched 9,700 km (6,000 miles) to set up Communist headquarters in safety. Mao finally took control of China in 1949.

The marchers had to make their way over steep mountains and through rocky gorges

Over three-quarters of the marchers died on the way

Fascism

HITLER
In Germany, the Nazi party came to power in 1933 under Adolf Hitler (1889–1945).

The fascist governments of Italy and Germany were opposed to democracy. They were led by dictators who took total control and ruthlessly suppressed opposition. Both regimes were keen to expand their power abroad. In 1935, Italy invaded Ethiopia. Germany occupied the Rhineland, took over part of Czechoslovakia, and annexed Austria. In 1936, Italy and Germany joined in a formal alliance.

Jewish homes and businesses were destroyed

ANTISEMITISM
From 1935, Jews in Germany were deprived of basic rights by law. Eventually, over six million Jews were killed.

The Nazi swastika symbol appeared everywhere

MUSSOLINI
Benito Mussolini (1883–1945) came to power in 1922, and by 1925 ruled Italy as a dictator. In 1940, he brought Italy into World War II on Germany's side.

PROPAGANDA
The Nazis used film, radio, the arts, and vast political rallies to brainwash people into accepting Nazi beliefs.

WORLD WAR II

IN 1939, WAR BROKE OUT in Europe after Germany invaded Poland. Then, in 1941, Japan attacked the US Navy base at Pearl Harbor, Hawaii, bringing the USA into the war. Once again, much of the world was at war.

BLITZKRIEG

By 1942, with its policy of "Blitzkrieg" (lightning war), Germany controlled most of Europe. The tide turned in 1943 with Allied rearmament and the US entry into the war.

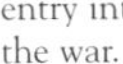

EUROPEAN WAR ZONE

The German army seemed unstoppable as they marched through Europe.

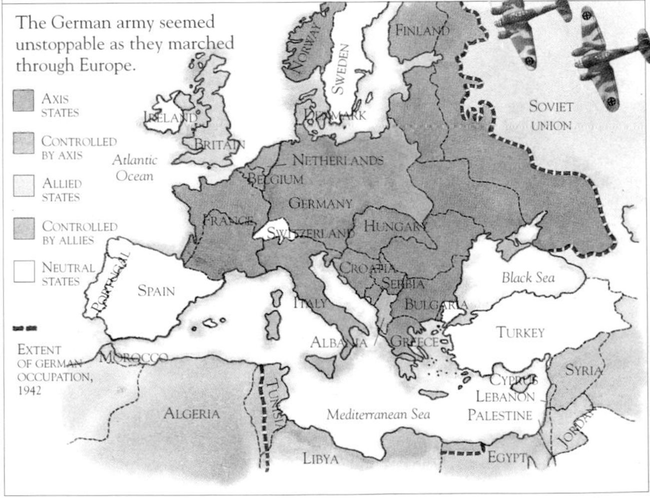

AXIS STATES

CONTROLLED BY AXIS

ALLIED STATES

CONTROLLED BY ALLIES

NEUTRAL STATES

EXTENT OF GERMAN OCCUPATION, 1942

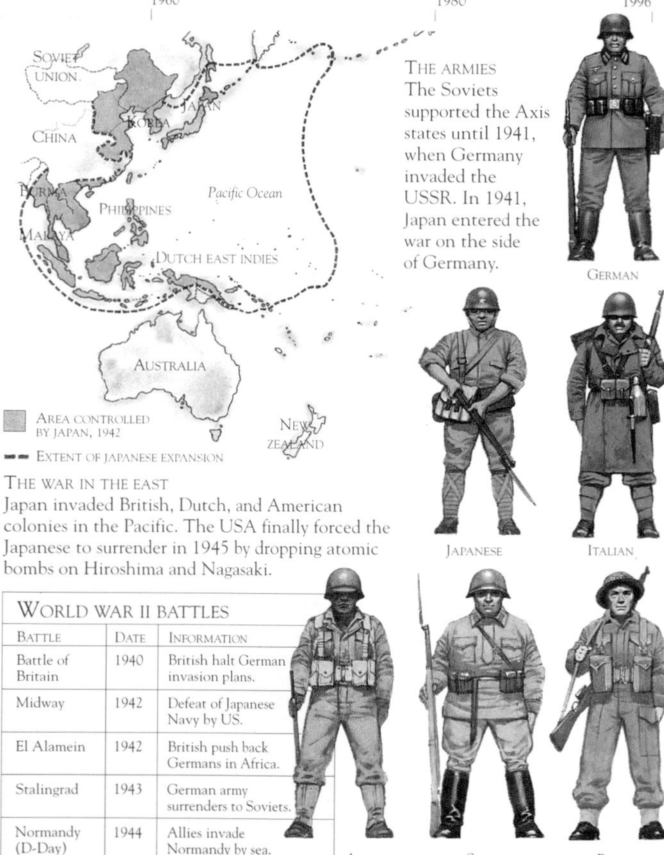

THE WAR IN THE EAST
Japan invaded British, Dutch, and American colonies in the Pacific. The USA finally forced the Japanese to surrender in 1945 by dropping atomic bombs on Hiroshima and Nagasaki.

THE ARMIES
The Soviets supported the Axis states until 1941, when Germany invaded the USSR. In 1941, Japan entered the war on the side of Germany.

GERMAN

JAPANESE

ITALIAN

AMERICAN

SOVIET

BRITISH

WORLD WAR II BATTLES

BATTLE	DATE	INFORMATION
Battle of Britain	1940	British halt German invasion plans.
Midway	1942	Defeat of Japanese Navy by US.
El Alamein	1942	British push back Germans in Africa.
Stalingrad	1943	German army surrenders to Soviets.
Normandy (D-Day)	1944	Allies invade Normandy by sea.

The aftermath of war

After the German surrender in May 1945, Germany was initially divided into four zones, each controlled by one of the Allied powers, Britain, France, the Soviet Union, and the USA. In 1949, the three western sectors were merged to become West Germany. The Soviet sector became a communist republic, East Germany.

BERLIN AIRLIFT
Berlin in East Germany was also divided into four sectors. In 1948, the USSR blockaded the city, preventing Westerners from bringing in supplies by land. Supplies were brought in by air for five months.

DESTRUCTION OF CITIES
Many cities had been badly damaged in air raids, and millions of civilians had lost their lives. After the war, cities had to be restored.

Many unstable buildings were demolished

Houses had been ripped apart, leaving many people homeless

Death toll	
Country	Deaths
USA	298,000
Britain	357,000
Italy	395,000
Japan	1,972,000
Germany	4,200,000
Soviet Union	18,000,000

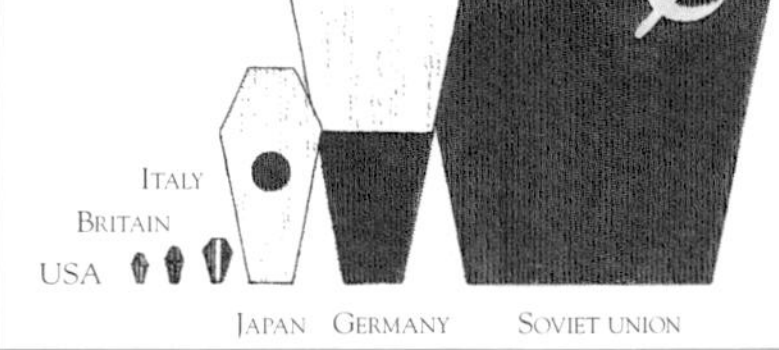

New industry
The industry of Japan and Germany had been badly hit by the war. The West gave economic aid to these countries to help them rebuild their industry.
As Japan and Germany's economies rapidly expanded, they once more became leading industrial powers.

The EEC
- In 1957, Belgium, France, Italy, Luxembourg, the Netherlands, and West Germany formed the European Economic Community, to remove trade barriers within Europe.
- The organization now has several more members, and is called the European Union. It has its own parliament with representatives from every member.

The united nations
In 1945, the United Nations (UN) was established with the aim of preventing future wars. The UN promotes human rights, encourages good relations between countries, and tries to find solutions to the world's problems.

THE COLD WAR

AFTER THE WAR, there was a clear split between the democratic West and the communist East. The USA and western Europe formed the North Atlantic Treaty Organization (NATO) to defend themselves from possible attack from the USSR and eastern Europe, who formed the Warsaw Pact. The two sides kept an uneasy peace in a situation known as the Cold War.

WEAPONS
Both sides stockpiled and tested conventional and nuclear weapons. They did not actually fight, but conflicts such as the Vietnam War were, in fact, struggles between East and West.

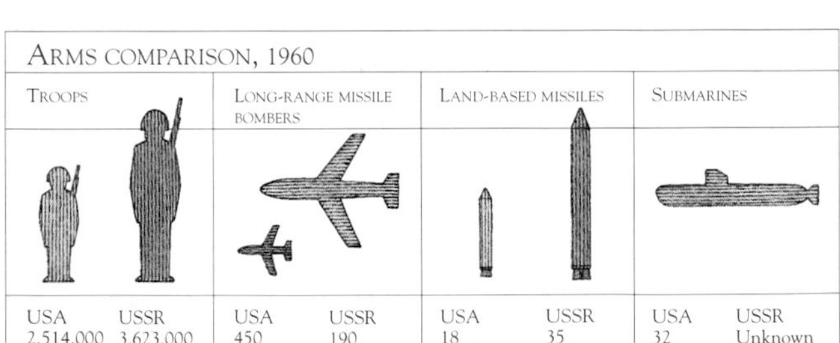

ARMS COMPARISON, 1960

TROOPS		LONG-RANGE MISSILE BOMBERS		LAND-BASED MISSILES		SUBMARINES	
USA	USSR	USA	USSR	USA	USSR	USA	USSR
2,514,000	3,623,000	450	190	18	35	32	Unknown

CONFLICTS AND CRISES		
COUNTRY	DATE	INFORMATION
Korea	1950–1953	South Korea, supported by the United Nations, fought North Korea, supported by communist China.
Cuba	1962	Communist Cuban leader Fidel Castro (b.1926) allowed the Soviet Union to build missile bases in Cuba. The USA blockaded Cuba, forcing the Soviets to remove the bases.
Vietnam	1965–1975	The USA, Australia, and New Zealand helped South Vietnam fight communist North Vietnam. In 1973, the Western allies withdrew. North Vietnam won the war in 1975.

VIETNAM WAR HELICOPTERS

The Space Race

In 1957, the Soviet Union surprised the world by launching Sputnik 1, the first artificial satellite. They launched the first manned space flight in 1961. In response, the USA stepped up their plans for space exploration. The Space Race was on.

SPUTNIK 1, THE FIRST ARTIFICIAL SATELLITE

THE FINAL FRONTIER
The USA organized a space programme that led to a manned landing on the Moon in 1969 (right). Meanwhile the Soviets concentrated on unmanned landings and the construction of Earth-orbiting space stations.

INDEPENDENCE MOVEMENTS

AFTER THE WAR, many countries that had been ruled by European powers gained independence. The new nations struggled to create their own systems of government, build up industry and trade, and cope with internal divisions. They relied on loans from richer nations, leading to a problem of long-term debt.

INDIAN INDEPENDENCE
Britain finally granted India independence after World War II. Indian leaders wanted to create a united country for both Hindus and Muslims, but most Muslims preferred to form a separate state. When the British left in 1947, the Muslim country of Pakistan was created to the north of the independent India.

CELEBRATION
Independence was often the result of a long period of struggle. Huge celebrations followed, like this one in Algeria.

CIVIL WARS
Most new African states had little unity because their borders were based on ones that had been drawn up by colonial powers. As a result, civil wars often broke out soon after independence.

African independence

Country	Flag	Date	Former ruler	Information
Ghana		1957	Britain	Corruption and coups dogged Ghana's government after independence.
Congo		1960	France	Independence was followed by civil war, and the Congo's first president was assassinated.
Mauritania		1960	France	The first president was overthrown by a military coup in 1978.
Nigeria		1960	Britain	Nigeria has been under almost constant military rule since independence.
Senegal		1960	France	The country was ruled under a virtual one-party government until the 1980s.
Algeria		1962	France	Independence was negotiated after an armed rebellion and a period of unrest.
Uganda		1962	Britain	A turbulent post-independence period led to over a million deaths.
Kenya		1963	Britain	Kenya was ruled as a one-party state until the first free elections in 1992.
Angola		1975	Portugal	Angola has been in an almost constant state of civil war since 1975.
Mozambique		1975	Portugal	Civil war, debt, and poor food supplies have led to famine and poverty.
Zimbabwe		1980	Britain	The black majority finally defeated the white minority and won independence.

South Africa

For the second half of the 20th century, South Africa was governed under the apartheid system which deprived non-white people of basic human rights. The main opposition to apartheid was organized by the African National Congress (ANC), which was banned in 1960. ANC leader Nelson Mandela (b.1918) was imprisoned from 1964 to 1989. Following general elections in 1994, Mandela led the first ANC government.

Protest and Change

THE 1950s AND 1960s saw many groups protesting against discrimination and campaigning for their rights. As a result, many important social changes began in this period, with black people in the USA and women in the Western world gaining more rights. This process of change is still continuing today.

MARTIN LUTHER KING

Civil rights

In the USA, leaders such as Martin Luther King and Malcolm X campaigned for the rights of black people. The lot of black Americans gradually began to improve.

USA civil rights

- In 1964, the Civil Rights Act protected racial minorities.
- The 1965 Voting Rights Act affirmed the right of black Americans to register to vote.
- Malcolm X (b.1925) was assassinated in 1965. King (b.1929) was shot dead in 1968.

Soviet tanks rumbled into Prague in August 1968

The Czech people were powerless

The Prague Spring

In 1968, the USSR invaded the Czech capital, Prague. The Soviets were afraid that liberal reforms made by the Czech government might weaken the Warsaw Pact.

Social changes

Many people wanted to transform society in the 1960s. While some groups began to assert their rights, others tried to "drop out" of society, living in peaceful communes, growing food, and sharing their belongings. Many also became worried about the threat of nuclear weapons.

The White House
REPEAL ABORTION LAWS N.O.W.
PASS the EQUAL RIGHTS AMENDMENT N.O.W.
Best kept secret since 1923... THE EQUAL RIGHTS AMENDMENT N.O.W. demands passage this year!

SEXUAL EQUALITY
The women's movement had four basic demands: equal opportunities in work and education, equal pay, free childcare, and free contraception and abortion.

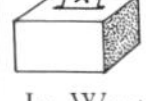

ELECTORAL RIGHTS
In Western countries today, most adults have the right to vote for the government of their choice. Until the 1990s, a single party system operated in the communist countries of Eastern Europe, so that even if voting was possible, the choice was severely limited.

THE CULTURAL REVOLUTION
Chinese leader Mao Tse-tung carried out his own Cultural Revolution from 1966. Many universities were closed, and teachers and students were forced to work on the land. Young people were encouraged to join the Red Guards who promoted Mao's policies and attacked those who disagreed.

Middle East Crises

SINCE WORLD WAR II, the Middle East has been one of the world's trouble spots. Disputes between the Jewish state of Israel and her Arab neighbours have dogged the Middle East since Israel was set up in 1948. Millions of Palestinians who used to live in the area are now refugees in other Arab nations. Meanwhile, there have been other conflicts over oil, territory, and religion.

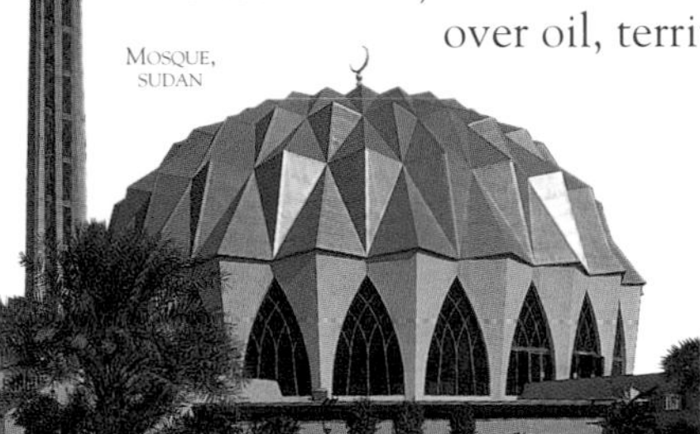

MOSQUE, SUDAN

RELIGIOUS STRUGGLES
Judaism, Christianity, and Islam all have their origins in the Middle East. All three consider certain places in Israel, such as Jerusalem, to be important holy sites.

OIL
Control of the world's oil supply has been a major factor in Middle Eastern wars, and has given the area considerable world power.

BLACK GOLD
Oil is the Middle East's most valuable natural resource. Major oil production in the region began in the 1940s, and by the following decade the region was an important producer.

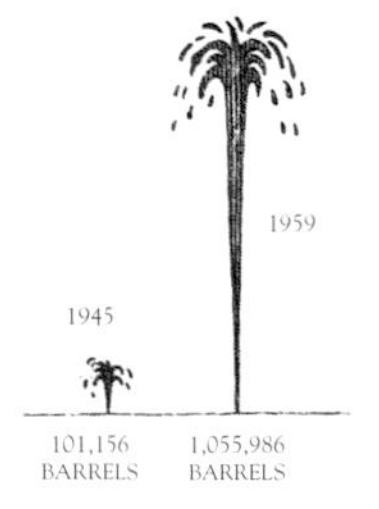

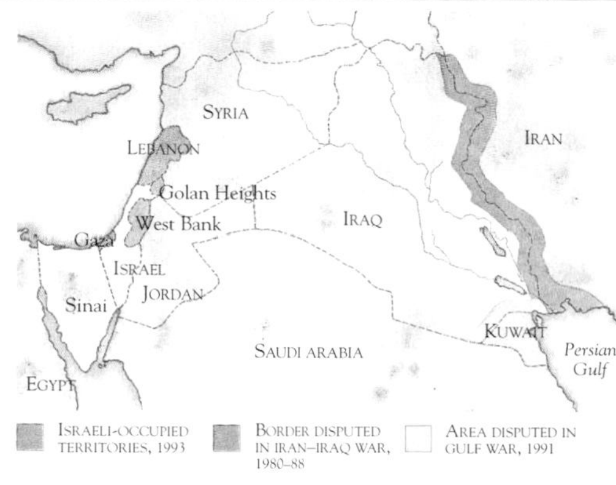

DISPUTED AREAS
This map shows the main areas that have been the scenes of recent conflicts in the Middle East. As well as disputes over oil and religious differences, there have been many clashes over territory in the region.

MIDDLE EAST CONFLICTS

WAR	DATE	INFORMATION
Six Day War	1967	Israeli troops seize the West Bank, the Gaza Strip, the Sinai Peninsula, and the Golan Heights, areas which are populated mainly by Palestinians.
Arab–Israeli War	1973	Egypt and Syria attack Israel, and an 18-day war leaves the conflict undecided. Peace treaty finally signed at Camp David, USA, 1979.
Iran–Iraq War	1980–1988	Iraqi forces attack the world's largest oil refinery at Abadab, Iran; Iraq gains some territory, but over 1 million people die; a ceasefire is overseen by the UN.
Lebanon	1982	Israel invades Lebanon and lays siege to the capital, Beirut, destroying the power base of the Palestine Liberation Organization (PLO); PLO is forced to evacuate.
West Bank and Gaza	1987–1993	Palestinian uprising in Israeli-occupied territories, but is suppressed by Israel; in 1992, moves towards peace give Palestinians some control over their affairs.
Gulf War	1990–1991	Iraq invades neighbouring Kuwait; UN responds by sending troops to fight Iraq; defeated Iraqis set fire to many oil-wells as they retreat, causing huge environmental damage.

THE WORLD TODAY

THROUGHOUT HISTORY, governments have risen and fallen, and countries have gained or lost power and territory. In recent years, the communist governments of the Soviet Union and Eastern Europe have made way for democratic systems. Some Asian countries have begun to grow in economic importance and world power.

GLASNOST
From 1985, Soviet leader Mikhail Gorbachev (b.1931) began to encourage change within the Soviet Union. His new policies of "Glasnost" (openness) and "Perestroika" (reconstruction) led to the break-up of the USSR.

TORN SOVIET FLAG
The Soviet Union ceased to exist in 1991.

THE COLLAPSE OF COMMUNISM
In 1989, communist governments in Czechoslovakia, Hungary, Romania, and East Germany all fell. The Berlin Wall was taken down in December 1989, paving the way for Germany to be reunited into a single nation.

One world

Today's world seems smaller than it did in the past. Wars concern not just the fighting parties, but also negotiators and peace-keepers from the UN. Crises such as famines involve international aid. Doctors all over the world are searching for cures for diseases such as AIDS. Environmental problems concern the whole planet and must be tackled globally.

CLEAN ENERGY
The world's dependence on fossil fuels such as coal, oil, and gas has caused environmental pollution and even damaged the atmosphere. New, clean energy sources include tidal power, solar power, and wind power.

TODAY'S INNOVATIONS

HOME VIDEO RECORDER
The first video recorders for use at home appeared in the 1970s.

VIDEO RECORDER

COMPUTERS
The early 1980s brought desk-top computers that were more powerful than the huge machines of the 1960s and 1970s.

MODERN COMPUTER

TEST-TUBE BABIES
The first baby conceived outside its mother's body was born in 1978.

TEST TUBE AND SYRINGE

THE POWER OF THE PACIFIC RIM
The economies of Hong Kong, Taiwan, Singapore, and South Korea have expanded, learning from Japan's success, and benefiting from low labour costs.

Coelder
poorte
kirch
Sea

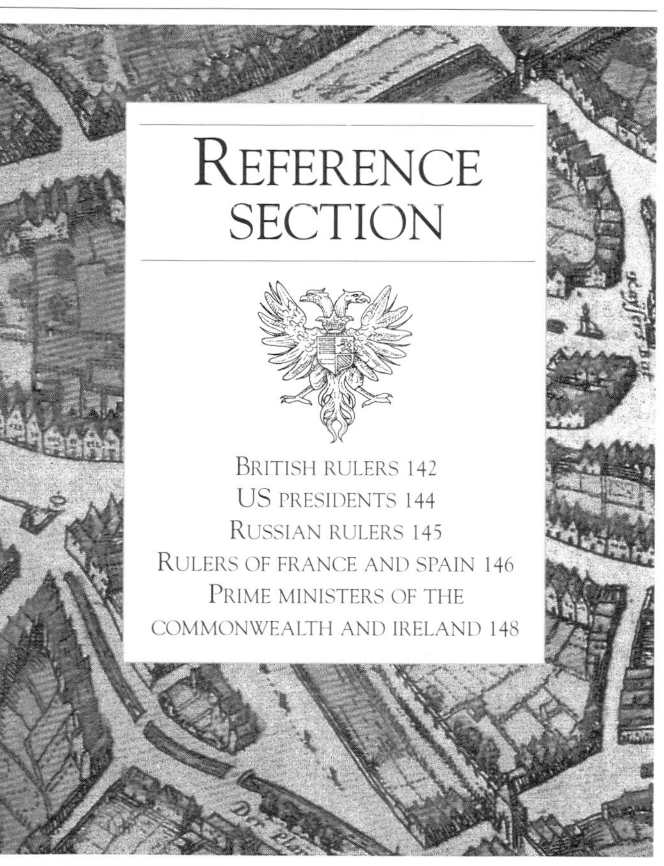

REFERENCE SECTION

BRITISH RULERS

THESE LISTS contain the monarchs of England and Scotland up until the early 17th century, and the joint British monarchs from then on.

MONARCHS OF ENGLAND

SAXON

1042–66	Edward the Confessor
1066	Harold II

NORMAN

1066–87	William I, the Conqueror
1087–1100	William II
1100–35	Henry I
1135–54	Stephen

PLANTAGENET

1154–89	Henry II
1189–99	Richard I, the Lionheart
1199–1216	John
1216–72	Henry III
1272–1307	Edward I
1307–27	Edward II
1327–77	Edward III
1377–99	Richard II

LANCASTER

1399–1413	Henry IV
1413–22	Henry V
1422–61	Henry VI

YORK

1461–83	Edward IV
1483	Edward V
1483–85	Richard III

TUDOR

1485–1509	Henry VII
1509–47	Henry VIII
1547–53	Edward VI
1553–58	Mary I
1558–1603	Elizabeth I

MONARCHS OF SCOTLAND

1306–29	Robert I, the Bruce
1329–71	David II

STUART

1371–90	Robert II
1390–1406	Robert III
1406–37	James I
1437–60	James II
1460–88	James III
1488–1513	James IV
1513–42	James V
1542–67	Mary, Queen of Scots
1567–1625	James VI

MONARCHS OF BRITAIN

STUART

1603–25	James I (VI of Scotland)
1625–49	Charles I

1649–60 COMMONWEALTH

STUART

1660–85	Charles II
1685–88	James II
1689–94	Mary II
1689–1702	William III
1702–14	Anne

HANOVER

1714–27	George I
1727–60	George II
1760–1820	George III
1820–30	George IV
1830–37	William IV
1837–1901	Victoria

SAXE-COBURG

1901–10	Edward VII

WINDSOR

1910–36	George V
1936	Edward VIII
1936–52	George VI
1952–	Elizabeth II

British Prime Ministers

1721–42	Robert Walpole
1742–43	Earl of Wilmington
1743–54	Henry Pelham
1754–56	Duke of Newcastle
1756–57	Duke of Devonshire
1757–62	Duke of Newcastle
1762–63	Earl of Bute
1763–65	George Grenville
1765–66	Marquess of Rockingham
1766–68	Earl of Chatham, Pitt the Elder
1768–70	Duke of Grafton
1770–82	Lord North
1782	Marquess of Rockingham
1782–83	Earl of Shelburne
1783	Duke of Portland
1783–1801	William Pitt, the Younger
1801–04	Henry Addington
1804–06	William Pitt, the Younger
1806–07	Lord Grenville
1807–09	Duke of Portland
1809–12	Spencer Perceval
1812–27	Earl of Liverpool
1827	George Canning
1827–28	Viscount Goderich
1828–30	Duke of Wellington
1830–34	Earl Grey
1834	Viscount Melbourne
1834–35	Robert Peel
1835–41	Viscount Melbourne
1841–46	Robert Peel
1846–52	Lord John Russell
1852	Earl of Derby
1852–55	Earl of Aberdeen
1855–58	Viscount Palmerston
1858–59	Earl of Derby
1859–65	Viscount Palmerston
1865–66	Earl Russell
1866–68	Earl of Derby
1868	Benjamin Disraeli
1868–74	William Gladstone
1874–80	Benjamin Disraeli
1880–85	William Gladstone
1885–86	Marquess of Salisbury
1886	William Gladstone
1886–92	Marquess of Salisbury
1892–94	William Gladstone
1894–95	Earl of Rosebery
1895–1902	Marquess of Salisbury
1902–05	Arthur Balfour
1905–08	Henry Campbell-Bannerman
1908–16	Herbert Asquith
1916–22	David Lloyd-George
1922–23	Andrew Bonar Law
1923–24	Stanley Baldwin
1924	James Ramsay-Macdonald
1924–29	Stanley Baldwin
1929–35	James Ramsay-Macdonald
1935–37	Stanley Baldwin
1937–40	Neville Chamberlain
1940–45	Winston Churchill
1945–51	Clement Attlee
1951–55	Winston Churchill
1955–57	Anthony Eden
1957–63	Harold Macmillan
1963–64	Sir Alec Douglas-Home
1964–70	Harold Wilson
1970–74	Edward Heath
1974–76	Harold Wilson
1976–79	James Callaghan
1979–90	Margaret Thatcher
1990–	John Major

US PRESIDENTS

AFTER THE American Revolution, George Washington became the first President of the United States. Presidents serve a term of four years and, since 1951, may only serve for two terms.

GEORGE WASHINGTON

ABRAHAM LINCOLN

FRANKLIN D. ROOSEVELT

STATUE OF LIBERTY

PRESIDENTS OF THE USA

Years	President
1789–97	George Washington
1797–1801	John Adams
1801–09	Thomas Jefferson
1809–17	James Madison
1817–25	James Monroe
1825–29	John Quincy Adams
1829–37	Andrew Jackson
1837–41	Martin van Buren
1841	William H. Harrison
1841–45	John Tyler
1845–49	James K. Polk
1849–50	Zachary Taylor
1850–53	Millard Fillmore
1853–57	Franklin Pierce
1857–61	James Buchanan
1861–65	Abraham Lincoln
1865–69	Andrew Johnson
1869–77	Ulysses S. Grant
1877–81	Rutherford B. Hayes
1881	James A. Garfield
1881–85	Chester A. Arthur
1885–89	Grover S. Cleveland
1889–93	Benjamin Harrison
1893–97	Grover S. Cleveland
1897–1901	William McKinley
1901–09	Theodore Roosevelt
1909–13	William H. Taft
1913–21	Woodrow Wilson
1921–23	Warren G. Harding
1923–29	Calvin Coolidge
1929–33	Herbert Hoover
1933–45	Franklin D. Roosevelt
1945–53	Harry S. Truman
1953–61	Dwight D. Eisenhower
1961–63	John F. Kennedy
1963–69	Lyndon B. Johnson
1969–74	Richard Nixon
1974–77	Gerald Ford
1977–81	James Carter
1981–89	Ronald Reagan
1989–93	George Bush
1993–	William J. Clinton

RUSSIAN RULERS

RUSSIAN RULERS have traditionally been known by the title Tsar, which means emperor and comes from the Roman title Caesar. In 1917, Russia became part of the Union of Soviet Socialist Republics (USSR), which lasted until 1992.

RUSSIAN MONARCHS

1462–1505	Ivan III, the Great
1505–33	Basil III
1533–84	Ivan IV, the Terrible
1584–98	Fyodor I
1598–1605	Boris Gudunov
1605	Fyodor II
1605–06	Demetrius
1606–10	Basil (IV) Shuiski
1610–13	INTERREGNUM
1613–45	Michael Romanov
1645–76	Alexis
1676–82	Fyodor III
1682–89	Ivan V and Peter I, the Great
1689–1725	Peter I, the Great
1725–27	Catherine I
1727–30	Peter II
1730–40	Anna
1740–41	Ivan VI
1741–62	Elizabeth
1762	Peter III
1762–96	Catherine II, the Great
1796–1801	Paul I
1801–25	Alexander I
1825–55	Nicholas I
1855–81	Alexander II
1881–94	Alexander III
1894–1917	Nicholas II

CATHERINE THE GREAT

VLADIMIR LENIN

LEADERS OF THE USSR

1917–22	Vladimir Lenin
1922–53	Joseph Stalin
1953–64	Nikita Krushchev
1964–82	Leonid Brezhnev
1982–84	Yuri Andropov
1984–85	Konstantin Chernenko
1985–92	Mikhail Gorbachev
1992–	Boris Yeltsin

KREMLIN CATHEDRAL OF THE ANNUNCIATION

RULERS OF FRANCE AND SPAIN

FRENCH MONARCHS and republican leaders are listed from the 10th century onwards. Spanish rulers are listed from the 15th century, when Spain was united under Ferdinand and Isabella.

FRENCH MONARCHS

CAROLINGIAN

936–954	Louis IV
954–986	Lothair
986–987	Louis V

LOUIS XIV

CAPET

987–996	Hugh Capet
996–1031	Robert II
1031–60	Henry I
1060–1108	Philip I
1108–37	Louis VI
1137–80	Louis VII
1180–1223	Philip II
1223–26	Louis VIII
1226–70	Louis IX
1270–85	Philip III
1285–1314	Philip IV
1314–16	Louis X
1316	John I
1316–22	Philip V
1322–28	Charles IV

NAPOLEON I

VALOIS

1328–50	Philip VI
1350–64	John II
1364–80	Charles V
1380–1422	Charles VI
1422–61	Charles VII
1461–83	Louis XI
1483–98	Charles VIII
1498–1515	Louis XII
1515–47	Francis I
1547–59	Henry II
1559–60	Francis II
1560–74	Charles IX
1574–89	Henry III

BOURBON

1589–1610	Henry IV
1610–43	Louis XIII
1643–1715	Louis XIV
1715–74	Louis XV
1774–92	Louis XVI

1792–1804	FIRST REPUBLIC

FIRST EMPIRE

1804–14	Napoleon I

BOURBON

1814–24	Louis XVIII
1824–30	Charles X
1830–48	Louis Philippe

1848–52	SECOND REPUBLIC

SECOND EMPIRE

1852–70	Napoleon III

French presidents

Third republic

1871–73 Adolphe Thiers
1873–79 Patrice de MacMahon
1879–87 Jules Grévy
1887–94 Marie François Sadi Carnot
1894–95 Jean Casimir-Périer
1895–99 François Félix Faure
1899–1906 Émile Loubet
1906–13 Armand Fallières
1913–20 Raymond Poincaré
1920 Paul Deschanel
1920–24 Alexandre Millerand
1924–31 Gaston Doumergue
1931–32 Paul Doumer
1932–40 Albert Lebrun

Vichy government

1940–44 Henri Philippe Pétain

Provisional government

1944–46 Charles de Gaulle
1946 Félix Gouin
1946 Georges Bidault
1946 Léon Blum

Fourth republic

1947–54 Vincent Auriol
1954–59 René Coty

Fifth republic

1959–66 Charles de Gaulle
1969–74 Georges Pompidou
1974–81 Valéry Giscard d'Estaing
1981–1995 François Mitterand
1995– Jacques Chirac

Spanish monarchs

1474–1504 Isabella of Castille
1479–1516 Ferdinand II of Aragon

Habsburg

1516–56 Charles I
1556–98 Philip II
1598–1621 Philip III
1621–65 Philip IV
1665–1700 Charles II

Isabella of Castille

Bourbon

1700–24 Philip V (abdicated)
1724 Louis I
1724–46 Philip V (restored)
1746–59 Ferdinand VI
1759–88 Charles III
1788–1808 Charles IV
1808 Ferdinand VII
1808–13 Joseph Bonaparte
1814–33 Ferdinand VII
1833–68 Isabella II
1870–73 Amadeus of Savoy

1873–74 First republic

Bourbon

1874–85 Alfonso XII
1885–86 Maria Cristina (Regent)
1886–1931 Alfonso XIII

1931–39 Second republic

1939–75 Francisco Franco (Dictator)

Bourbon

1975– Juan Carlos

PRIME MINISTERS OF THE COMMONWEALTH AND IRELAND

THESE LISTS SHOW the prime ministers of Australia, Ireland, Canada, and New Zealand from the time these countries became independent from Britain.

AUSTRALIAN PRIME MINISTERS

1901–03	Edmund Barton
1903–04	Alfred Deakin
1904	John C. Watson
1904–05	George Houston Reid
1905–08	Alfred Deakin
1908–09	Andrew Fisher
1909–10	Alfred Deakin
1910–13	Andrew Fisher
1913 14	Joseph Cook
1914–15	Andrew Fisher
1915–23	William M. Hughes
1923–29	Stanley M. Bruce
1929–32	James H. Scullin'
1932–39	Joseph A. Lyons
1939	Earle Page
1939–41	Robert Gordon Menzies
1941	Arthur William Fadden
1941–45	John J. Curtin
1945	Francis M. Forde
1945–49	Joseph Benedict Chifley
1949–66	Robert Gordon Menzies
1966–67	Harold Edward Holt
1967–68	John McEwen
1968 71	John Grey Gorton
1971–72	William McMahon
1972–75	E. Gough Whitlam
1975–83	J. Malcolm Fraser
1983–91	Robert Hawke
1991–	Paul J. Keating

IRISH PRIME MINISTERS

1922	Arthur Griffith
1922	Michael Collins
1922–32	William Cosgrave
1932–48	Eamonn de Valera
1948–51	John Aloysius Costello
1951–54	Eamonn de Valera
1954–57	John Aloysius Costello
1957–59	Eamonn de Valera
1959–66	Sean Lemass
1966–73	Jack Lynch
1973–77	Liam Cosgrave
1977–79	Jack Lynch
1979–81	Charles Haughey
1981–82	Garrett Fitzgerald
1982	Charles Haughey
1982–87	Garrett Fitzgerald
1987–92	Charles Haughey
1992–94	Albert Reynolds
1994–	John Bruton

Canadian Prime Ministers

1867–73	John A. Macdonald
1873–78	Alexander Mackenzie
1878–91	John A. Macdonald
1891–92	John J. C. Abbott
1892–94	John Sparrow Thompson
1894–96	Mackenzie Bowell
1896	Charles Tupper
1896–1911	Wilfred Laurier
1911–20	Robert Laird Borden
1920–21	Arthur Meighen
1921–26	W. L. Mackenzie King
1926	Arthur Meighen
1926–30	W. L. Mackenzie King
1930–35	Richard Bedford Bennett
1935–48	W. L. Mackenzie King
1948–57	Louis St Laurent
1957–63	John G. Diefenbaker
1963–68	Lester Bowles Pearson
1968–79	Pierre Elliott Trudeau
1979–80	Charles Joseph Clark
1980–84	Pierre Elliott Trudeau
1984	John Napier Turner
1984–93	Martin Brian Mulroney
1994	Kim Campbell
1994–	Jean Chrétien

New Zealand Prime Ministers

1856	Henry Sewell
1856	William Fox
1856–61	Edward William Stafford
1861–62	William Fox
1862–63	Alfred Domett
1863–64	Frederick Whitaker
1864–65	Frederick Aloysius Weld
1865–69	Edward William Stafford
1869–72	William Fox
1872	Edward William Stafford
1872–73	George M. Waterhouse
1873	William Fox
1873–75	Julius Vogel
1875–76	Daniel Pollen
1876	Julius Vogel
1876–77	Harry Albert Atkinson
1877–79	George Grey
1879–82	John Hall
1882–83	Frederick Whitaker
1883–84	Harry Albert Atkinson
1884	Robert Stout
1884	Harry Albert Atkinson
1884–87	Robert Stout
1887–91	Harry Albert Atkinson
1891–93	John Ballance
1893–1906	Richard John Seddon
1906	William Hall-Jones
1906–12	Joseph George Ward
1912	Thomas Mackenzie
1912–25	William Ferguson Massey
1925	Francis Henry Dillon Bell
1925–28	Joseph Gordon Coates
1928–30	Joseph George Ward
1930–35	George William Forbes
1935–40	Michael J. Savage
1940–49	Peter Fraser
1949–57	Sidney J. Holland
1957	Keith J. Holyoake
1957–60	Walter Nash
1960–72	Keith J. Holyoake
1972	John Marshall
1972–74	Norman Kirk
1974–75	Wallace E. Rowling
1975–84	Robert D. Muldoon
1984–89	David Lange
1989–90	Geoffrey Palmer
1990	Michael Moore
1990–	James Bolger

Resources

Local museums and libraries provide the most useful historical resources. They will give you information about your area and should be able to tell you about local history societies and other organizations that offer further information. From the hundreds of historical museums, a small selection is listed below. Also listed are the addresses of organizations which look after many heritage sites.

Organizations

English Heritage
Fortress House
23 Saville Row
London W1X 1RB
National organization that looks after ancient monuments, especially castles and prehistoric remains

National Trust
36 Queen Anne's Gate
London SW1H 9AS
National charity for places of historic interest and natural importance, including many country houses

Museums

American Museum
Claverton Manor
Bath
Avon BA2 7BD
Life in North America from the 17th to the 19th centuries

Black Country Museum
Tipton Road
Dudley
West Midlands DY1 4SO
Open-air museum of West Midlands life in the 19th and early 20th centuries

British Museum
Great Russell Street
London WC1
The national museum, with collections from all historical periods

Buckler's Hard Maritime Museum
Heritage Centre
Buckler's Hard
Brockenhurst
Hampshire SO42 7ZN
18th-century ship-building village and museum of maritime history

Corinium Museum
Park Street
Cirencester
Gloucestershire GL7 2BX
Roman and Romano-British history

Gladstone Court Street Museum
Biggar
Strathclyde ML12 6DL
Reconstruction of Victorian shopping centre, library, and schoolroom

Great Western Railway Museum
Farringdon Road
Swindon
Wiltshire SN1 5BJ
Railway history

Historic Dockyard
Chatham
Kent ME4 4TE
Maritime history and ship-building

Imperial War Museum
Lambeth Road
London SE1 6HZ
Warfare and its effects during the 20th century

Ironbridge Gorge Museum
Ironbridge
Telford
Shropshire TF8 7SW
The industrial revolution

Jorvik Viking Centre
Coppergate
York YO1 1NT
Reconstructed Viking settlement

Liverpool Museum
William Brown Street
Liverpool L3 8EN
General museum covering wide range of historical periods

Mary Rose Exhibition and Ship Hall
HM Naval Base
Portsmouth
Hampshire PO1 3LX
Henry VIII's flagship, salvaged from the seabed, plus items found on board

Museum of London
London Wall
London EC2Y 5HN
History of the capital city from the earliest times to the present day

Museum of the Iron Age
6 Church Close
Andover SP10 1DP
Life during the Iron Age, including material from an important local hill fort

National Museum of Wales
Cathys Park
Cardiff
General museum covering wide range of historical periods

North of England Open Air Museum
Beamish
Co Durham
Living re-creation of life in northeast England at the turn of the century

Reading Museum of English Rural Life
University of Reading
Whiteknight
Reading
Berkshire RG6 2AG
Farming, crafts, and the countryside over the past 150 years

Royal Museum of Scotland
Chambers Street
Edinburgh EH1 1JF
General museum covering wide range of historical periods

Ulster Museum
Botanic Gardens
Belfast BT9 5AB
The archaeology, prehistory, and history of Northern Ireland

Wigan Pier
Wigan
Lancashire WN3 4EU
Living recreation of industrial life, including the largest mill steam engine

Victoria and Albert Museum
Cromwell Road
London SW7 2RL
Fine and applied art up to the present day

Glossary

Abdicate
(Of a monarch) to give up the throne voluntarily.

Absolute ruler
A monarch who has complete power over his or her subjects, and is not answerable to a government.

Ally
A state or person formally united with another, normally by means of a treaty.

Archaeology
The study of the material remains of past human cultures.

Artefact
An object made by a person, such as a tool or a work of art.

Barbarian
An uncivilized or primitive person; a member of one of the various peoples who took over after the fall of the Roman Empire.

City-state
A city with its own independent government.

Civilization
A complex and well-developed society that usually has large cities, a system of government, an organized religion, and a form of writing.

Civil service
The staff responsible for the administration of a government, such as collection of taxes.

Civil war
A conflict between groups within one nation or state.

Colony
Territory that is at some distance from the country that governs it. People from the governing country who live in a colony are called colonists.

Constitution
An outline of the basic principles by which a nation is governed and the key rights of the citizens.

Culture
The ideas, beliefs, and knowledge of a particular people.

Democracy
Government by the representatives of the people, chosen by free election.

Depression
An economic slump, generally featuring low investment, high unemployment, and low production levels.

Dictator
An absolute and usually tyrannical ruler.

Discrimination
The singling out of a group for unfair or unfavourable treatment, usually because of race, sex, or membership of a specific minority.

Dynasty
A group of rulers of the same family.

Economy
The range of activities concerned with producing, selling, and consuming goods and services within a nation.

Emigration
The process of leaving one's native country to settle in another.

Empire
A collection of peoples, areas, or former states under the rule of one person (the emperor).

Epidemic
The widespread occurrence of a disease.

Famine
An acute shortage of food.

Government
The way in which a country is ruled; the group of people who rule (govern) a country.

Heretic
A person who disagrees with some of the beliefs of the local religion. A heretic's beliefs are known as heresy.

Human rights
The basic rights that a person is entitled to, such as justice and freedom.

Innovation
The introduction of something such as a new method or device.

Legal system
The laws of a country; the system of police, courts, lawyers, and judges who enforce these laws.

Liberty
The power of individuals to think, speak, and make choices without unfair government control.

Monarch
A ruler, usually a king, queen, emperor, or empress.

Nationalist
A person who believes in and sometimes fights for the right of an area to become an independent nation.

Parliament
The national assembly, usually elected democratically, that passes the laws of a country.

Policy
A system of ideas or plans of a particular country or government.

Reform
A change in law or policy intended to bring about an improvement.

Regime
A system of government.

Republic
A system of government in which the head of the country is elected or nominated.

Revolution
The overthrow of a country's government by a group of its people; an extreme change in the way things are done.

Sacrifice
Giving up one thing for another, for example giving an offering in return for a god's favour.

Scribe
A person who made hand-written copies of documents before the invention of printing.

Serf
A worker in feudal Europe who was not allowed to leave the land he worked on.

Siege
A method of warfare involving surrounding a city or castle, cutting off supplies, and attacking.

Society
A group of peoples with distinctive beliefs, aims, and cultural traditions.

Technology
The practical use of scientific and mechanical skills.

Territory
Land governed by a particular state or ruler.

Index

Acknowledgements

Dorling Kindersley would like to thank: Hilary Bird for the index; Robin Hunter and Martin Wilson for design assistance; Caroline Potts and John Stevenson for picture research.

Illustrations by: David Ashby, Peter Bailey, Russell Barnett, Steven Conlin, Peter Dennis (Linda Rogers Associations), Bill Donohoe, Eugene Fleury, Chris Forsey, Luigi Galante, Nick Harris, Nicholas Hewetson, Richard Hook (Linden Artists), Jason Lewis, Angus McBride (Linden Artists), Sergio Momo, Tony Mannis, Tony Morris, Sarah Ponder, Sallie Alane Reason, Sebastian Quigley, Rodney Shackell, Eric Thomas, John Woodcock.

Photographs by: Peter Anderson, Geoff Brightling, Andy Crawford, Geoff Dann, Philip Dowell, Mike Dunning, David Exton, Chas Howson, Colin Keates, Dave King, Andrew McRobb, Martin Plomer, Tim Ridley, Karl Shone, James Stevenson, Clive Streeter, Michel Zabé.

Picture Credits
t top; *c* centre; *b* bottom; *l* left; *r* right.

The publisher would like to thank the following for their kind permission to reproduce their photographs:

Ancient Art & Architecture/Ronald Sheridan 48br, 59tl; Ashmolean Museum, Oxford 1, 2br, 12tr, 25br, 36bl, 37br, 39cl, 41br, 42r, 43cr, tr, 70-71, 82-83c, 87br, 89tc; Bolton Metro Museum 10tr, 35tl; Bridgeman Art Library/Forbes Magazine Collection, New York 120br, Giraudon 60-61b, Kunsthistoriches Museum, Vienna 61cr, Vatican Museums & Galleries 77t; The British Library 44tr; The British Museum 107tl, 123br; Musée de L'Emperi 99tr, tc; The Horniman Museum 78l; The Image Bank/Guido Alberto Rossi 139br, Harald Sund 139tr; Imperial War Museum 108bc, 125t, br; Magnum Photos Ltd/Rene Burri: 129c, Marc Riboud: 132cr; Museum of London 11tr, 25tr, bl; Museum of the Moving Image 123cr; National Maritime Museum 3bl, 13br, 35b, 46b; National Museum of Denmark, Copenhagen 10cl, 62tl, 63tr; National Museum of Scotland 76c; National Railway Museum, York 90-91, 105tl; Natural History Museum 21bl; NASA 110-111, 131b Oslo Ship Museum 62br; Pitt Rivers Museum, Oxford 16-17, 65br, 84tl, 85br; Popperfoto 134c; Range Pictures Ltd/Bettmann 120c,122b, 124tr, 125bc, 130c 144l; /UPI 135c; Rex Features Ltd 136; /CTK 134b; /Jacques Witt 133b; Sipa Press 132bc, /Laski 138tr; Robert Wallis 138b; Royal Museum of Scotland 50b; Peter Sanders 136b; Science Museum, London 35b, 96b, 105br, cl, 107br; University Museum of Archaeology & Anthropology, Cambridge 20r, 26-27, 33tl, br, bc, 52-53, 66b; Wallace Collection, London 2tr, 68bl, 81tl, 83tl, 85c, 88tl, cr, 100tl, tr.

Every effort has been made to trace the copyright holders and we apologize in advance for any unintentional omissions. We would be pleased to insert the appropriate acknowledgement in any subsequent edition of this publication.